GENE WOLFE

MORE WILDSIDE CLASSICS

GENE WOLFE

by

JOAN GORDON

WILDSIDE PRESS

For my mother,
Edna K. Gordon

GENE WOLF

This edition published in 2006 by Wildside Press, LLC.
www.wildsidepress.com

CONTENTS

CITATIONS AND ABBREVIATIONS

Because science fiction tends to go in and out of print, I cite both page numbers of first editions (see primary bibliography) and chapter numbers of Wolfe's work. These citations occur parenthetically in the text and use the following abbreviations.

CA   The Citadel of the Autarch

CC   The Claw of the Conciliator

CO   The Castle of the Otter

DF   The Devil in a Forest

FH   The Fifth Head of Cerberus

GWBD   Gene Wolfe's Book of Days

OA   Operation ARES

P   Peace

SL   The Sword of the Lictor

ST   The Shadow of the Torturer

TIOD   The Island of Doctor Death and Other Stories and Other Stories

CHRONOLOGY OF LIFE AND WORKS

May 7, 1931--born in Brooklyn, NY
1933 — earliest memory, of running across green grass;
contracts polio without permanent effects.
1939 — goes to the New York World's Fair.
1941 — moves to Houston, Texas, to live for fourteen
years, after years of having moved every one or two
years.
1949 — graduates from Lamar High School in Houston, enters
Texas A. and M.
1951-1952 — writes for Texas A. and M. humor magazine.
1952 — drops out of Texas A. and M. and is drafted.
1953 — sent to Korea to fight in Korean War in April;
ceasefire in July.
1954 — discharged from the army, enters University of
Houston.
1956 — graduates from University of Houston with BSME;
hired by Procter and Gamble in Cincinnati, OH;
marries Rosemary Dietsch.
1957 — begins writing, theoretically to provide income for
buying furniture.
1958 — first child, Roy Emerson II (after Wolfe's father),
born.
1960 — second child, Madeleine, born.
1963 — third child, Therese Georgeanne, born.
1965 — sells first story, "The Dead Man," to Sir, and
first science-fiction story, "Mountains Like Mice,"
to If.
1966 — fourth child, Matthew Dietsch, born.
1967 — first Orbit publication, "The Changeling," in Orbit.
1970 — Operation ARES, first novel, published; "The Island
of Doctor Death and Other Stories" published in Orbit 7; first Nebula Award nomination (best short
story) for "The Island of Doctor Death and Other
Stories," which was second in voting to "No Award."
1972 — leaves Procter and Gamble and becomes editor of
Plant Engineering, Barrington, IL; The Fifth Head
of Cerberus, novella cycle, published.
1973 — father dies, wins Nebula Award (best novella) for
"The Death of Doctor Island"; receives first Hugo
nomination, for "The Fifth Head of Cerberus."
1975 — Peace, mainstream novel, published.

1976 — The Devil in a Forest, adolescent novel, published.
1977 — mother dies; wins Chicago Foundation for Literature Award (best novel) for Peace.
1978 — Rhysling Award (best long science-fiction poem) for "The Computer Iterates the Greater Trumps"; "Seven American Nights" published in Orbit 20.
1980 — The Island of Doctor Death and Other Stories and Other Stories, first short story collection, published; The Shadow of the Torturer, first volume of The Book of the New Sun, published.
1981 — wins World Fantasy Award (best novel) for The Shadow of the Torturer; Illinois Arts Council Award (best short story) for "In Looking Glass Castle"; The Claw of the Conciliator, second volume of The Book of the New Sun, published; Gene Wolfe's Book of Days, second short story collection, published.
1982 — wins Nebula Award (best novel) for The Claw of the Conciliator; The Sword of the Lictor, third volume of The Book of the New Sun, published; The Castle of the Otter published; The Citadel of the Autarch, fourth volume of The Book of the New Sun, published.

II

INTRODUCTION

Gene Wolfe writes elegant and evocative prose that refuses to fall clearly within a specific genre. Though he writes within the science-fiction network, Wolfe prefers to identify his writing as speculative fiction, and his preference reflects the variance of his work from traditional science fiction. His stories do not necessarily use science, nor do they always take place in a future or alternate world. Although it uses science and the future, his major work, the tetralogy The Book of the New Sun, has much of the feel of fantasy. Wolfe seldom stresses action or the mechanics of how things work.

Even when Wolfe's stories do use science-fictional devices and settings, they differ from most other science fiction in their emphasis on ambiguity, psychological narrative, and mood evocation. This emphasis has made him a writer more frequently appreciated by writers, critics, and scholars than by the mass of science-fiction readers.

Gene Wolfe is a clever man. He has a biting, ironic, swiftly-paced sense of humor; laces his conversation with puns; states his seldom mundane or predictable views unequivocally; and argues them stubbornly and well. When he chooses to ignore a question—he has little time for ignorant or prying questions—he does so with equal stubbornness and skill. In his speech and in his writing, he reveals his complexity, though seldom directly. His religious and political beliefs fit his character and writing: strong, complex, and hard to categorize. He is

a Catholic in the real communion-taking sense, which tells you a lot less than you think about my religious beliefs. . . . I believe in God, in the divinity of Christ and in the survival of the person. . . . Like every thinking person, I am still working out my beliefs.

Politically, I am a maverick. I agree with the far left on many issues, with the far right on others, with the center on still others. I distrust concentrations of power, whether political or economic. I am a strong environmentalist. I believe that we are higher creatures than we think we are, and that animals are closer to us than we believe.(1)

3

Though a reader can find some of Wolfe's politics and religious beliefs in his fiction, Wolfe is a private person who speaks little of his personal life and uses it only indirectly in his writing.

Wolfe, an only child, was born on May 7, 1931, in Brooklyn, New York, and for the first ten years of his life moved frequently--to Peoria, Illinois, and to Massachusetts, Ohio, and Iowa. When he reached fourth grade, the family settled down in Houston, which became "my home town, the place I was from."(2) Wolfe attended Texas A. and M. where he majored in mechanical engineering, "I suspect because someone told my father and me it was good thing to take until you made up your mind."(3) He dropped out of college in the middle of his junior year, 1952, and was drafted for the Korean War, serving in the infantry and seeing combat. In 1954, after he was discharged, Wolfe returned to Texas and completed his Bachelor of Science in Mechanical Engineering at the University of Houston on the GI Bill. Five months after his graduation and their reunion, Wolfe married Rosemary Dietsch, the little girl from Peoria with whom he had played when he was four. After graduation, Wolfe worked for sixteen years for Procter and Gamble in Cincinnati, Ohio; among his other projects, he designed the machine that forms Pringle's potato chips. He then left and became an editor of the trade journal, Plant Engineering, based in Barrington, Illinois, where he worked until his recent retirement to write full-time. Gene and Rosemary Wolfe live in Barrington and have four children: Roy, Madeleine, Therese, and Matthew.

This sketch of Wolfe's life suggests some of the material of his stories. An only child who spent the first years of his life moving around the country, he often writes of isolated children and uprooted adults. His short career at Texas A. and M., his army stint, and his years of working in industry suggest his stories of people trapped by regulation. The sketch cannot indicate why a man who holds down a full-time job and has a large family to care for drives himself to spend his leisure time writing five pages a day and why he has so many powerful stories to tell. The answer to these riddles lies within Wolfe's character, not as it is shaped by exterior events but as it shapes them. In an interview with Gardner Dozois in Xenolith One, Wolfe said, "I don't think fiction is a proper vehicle for philosophy except that the character's philosophy affects his actions."(4) Because Wolfe is the person he is, he writes no matter how difficult or inconvenient it might seem.

For any artist, a very unromantic attribute must accompany native genius for the talent to bloom; that is dis-

cipline. Discipline makes it possible for Gene Wolfe to
find the time to write. Though his full-time job and family
commitments didn't permit a rigid routine, Wolfe managed an
hour of writing each morning before he left for work and
another hour or two each evening. "I usually get in about
four hours of writing on Saturday and Sunday."(5) The
isolation of a basement study helps concentrate these hours.
   Concern for discipline also hones Wolfe's stories into
their characteristic tightness of structure and imagery:

> I write the piece all the way through, then
> start again at the beginning, then start again
> at the beginning. . . . Everything gets at least
> three drafts. Most things get four. A good
> many get four plus. I continue to revise until
> I begin to wonder if the changes I'm making are
> really improvements. . . . Then I stop and send
> out the piece. Whenever possible, I allow at
> least a week between revisions and I usually use
> that week to work on something else.(6)

Wolfe's artistry comes from both industry and inspiration,
as his stories come from both his life and his character.
   Though it is difficult to categorize Wolfe's works as
types of fiction—science fiction, science fantasy, fantasy,
new fiction, and so on—three main types emerge within his
body of works: (1) entertainments, and serious stories in
either a (2) sociological or (3) psychological vein.
Naturally, Wolfe as a person of complexity and indirection
does not write stories that fit tractably and exclusively
within these three categories; instead, his stories usually
contain more elements of one category than of the others,
and they align with the concerns and attributes of one sort
of writing more than with the others.
   A typical Wolfe entertainment is quite short, uses
puns and literary or historical allusions, has a surprise
ending, and, though it may treat a serious theme, remains
light in tone. Although a thorough understanding of the
story may require recognition of allusions and the skill to
catch puns and surprises, these stories typically end with a
definite closure, without suggestions of ambiguity either in
the stories' events or in the interpretations of them. They
are the most accessible of Wolfe's fictions. Most typical
of this sort of story are "Cues" (TIOD), "Car Sinister," and
"How I Lost the Second World War and Helped Turn Back the
German Invasion" (both in GWBD). The first is a brief story
summed up in the last line by a pun--in other words, a
semantic joke. The second and third stories build plots

around puns. Other stories, such as "La Befana" (TIOD), rely on the reader's recognition of allusion (here, to the Christmas story and to an Italian Christmas legend) and are less frivolous than the punning stories.

Wolfe's entertainments are reminiscent of Damon Knight's stories, especially Knight's classic "To Serve Man."(7) With both writers, skill lies in the wit and aptness with which puns are presented and surprises are sprung upon the reader. That Wolfe shares much with Damon Knight is not surprising: Wolfe's career has several links to Knight's. Wolfe has attended several sessions of The Milford Conference, run by Knight and his wife, Kate Wilhelm. Wolfe's stories have appeared in fourteen of the twenty-one Orbit anthologies, which Knight edited. Knight encouraged Wolfe, in 1966, to expand a short story, "The Laughter Outside at Night," into his first published novel, Operation ARES, which Knight then bought for Berkley. This encouragement may partly explain the dedication of The Fifth Head of Cerberus "to Damon Knight, who one well-remembered June evening in 1966 grew me from a bean." Wolfe describes Knight and Kate Wilhelm as "more or less the older brother and sister I never had."(8)

The entertainments, however, form a rather small proportion of Wolfe's production, especially as he represents it in his anthologies, The Island of Dr. Death and Other Stories and Other Stories and Gene Wolfe's Book of Days. They reveal Wolfe's tricky and cerebral humor, though they don't reflect further intricacies of his mind and writing. More strongly represented in the anthologies are Wolfe's sociological stories. Characteristically, these deal either with an ecological issue ("An Article about Hunting" in GWBD) or with the power of systems over the individual ("Forlesen," also in GWBD), or with both, as in Operation ARES. Their most common motif, reminiscent of Franz Kafka, is the minor bureaucrat lost in a confusing maze of societal rules and regulations that remain a mystery to the individual. Wolfe typically relates such stories in a flat, business-like tone that mimics the callous language of bureaucratic management or of environmental exploitation. Because Wolfe deals with the confusion of human beings coping with regulatory coldness and pointlessness, he employs ambiguity; we cannot be sure, any more than the protagonist can be, of the rules, motives, schemes, and decay that surround us or him. Such ambiguity, which precludes tidy closures to these stories, is an element strongly associated with almost all of Wolfe's work. It is an element which is, on the one hand, necessary to effectively document the worlds he envisions, and on the other

6

hand, upsetting to those science-fiction readers who expect and desire entertainments that end with a resolution.

Such ambiguity is even more pervasive in Wolfe's strongest works, his psychological stories. Though we can spot influences of Proust, Dickens, and Borges in these stories, Wolfe's most powerful and original voice resides in his psychological stories, and it is here that he makes his most valuable contribution to the elevation of science fiction to an important literary category. Wolfe's psychological stories build worlds from the minds of the characters who inhabit them. Wolfe shows us ways in which minds perceive worlds, strange or otherwise, rather than purporting to show objectively observable worlds that characters inhabit and to which they react. These psychological stories focus upon the workings of a mind rather than upon those of a planet, and this focus characterizes the strongest, largest and best-known portion of Wolfe's repertoire. Among them are his novella cycle, The Fifth Head of Cerberus, as well as other superb novellas, such as "Seven American Nights," "Tracking Song," and "The Island of Dr. Death and Other Stories" (in TIOD), his tetralogy The Book of the New Sun, his mainstream novel Peace, and many of his short stories.

These works show Wolfe at his most complex. Not only do they tend to incorporate motifs, themes, and stylistic devices common to his entertainments and his sociological stories, but they use many other devices as well to deal with universal yet quite personal issues. Lonely or disturbed children, alien or inverted myths and legends, and non-human sentient species confronting one another appear repeatedly to illustrate themes of isolation, memory, and the search for self and human identity. In these stories, Wolfe adopts a cool tone, recollecting emotion from a distance of time and space, even when the voice is that of a narrating protagonist. Such distance emphasizes the isolation of the character and the importance of memory in perception of events. Puns and allusions join with formal, archaic, or esoteric vocabulary, stylistic indirection, and compound-complex sentences to build distance, intricacy of vision, and ambiguity—all traits of Wolfe's most characteristic fiction.

The psychological stories deal with perceptions of reality, which vary with the state of mind of the perceiver. Wolfe shows these layers of reality by embedding stories within stories as many as six layers deep (Peace contains his most exuberant use of the technique) and by blending dream sequences with events that seem to be on a surface, empirical level. Wolfe lets dreams infect reality, as

7

Borges would say. He also uses metaphors to blur the dis-
tinction between imagination and empirical reality. He may
begin a metaphor in such a way as to make it seem a separate
story embedded in the main narrative. Then, he connects it
to a second story or circumstance, turning it into a
metaphor unconnected with the main narrative. The
metaphorical interludes may well be as vivid, as realistic,
as the perceptions in the main narrative which we had taken
to be the "real story." Finally, he metaphorically connects
the second embedded story with the main narrative and comes
round full circle. All these devices teach us that perceptions are all we know of reality and that perceptions change
according to the allusive, associative nature of the mind.

Wolfe's psychological stories are far from typical of
the science-fiction traditions and conventions. For readers
raised on Clarke, Asimov, and Heinlein, Wolfe's stories
don't "feel" like science fiction precisely because they de-
emphasize the empirical reality so many science-fiction
writers stress to give their concocted worlds credibility.
Some of the apparatuses of science fiction nevertheless
appear: Severian of The Shadow of the Torturer takes his
training in an abandoned space ship; The Fifth Head of Cerberus describes two alien planets; "Seven American Nights"
takes place in the future; "The Death of Dr. Island" uses
new technology. In spite of the apparatuses and because of
the angle of perception, Wolfe generally prefers to call his
work speculative fiction. Since the hard sciences--physics,
chemistry, and astronomy, for example--play such a small
role in his work, "science" isn't very descriptive, whereas
speculation, the question "what if," is vital to Wolfe's
fiction.

Not only is Gene Wolfe's speculative fiction atypical,
it is demanding as well, and demanding to a degree some
science-fiction readers find uncomfortable. The notion that
science fiction provides light, escapist reading has just
enough truth to make many of its readers expect stories
which contain straightforward, unadorned plots and style,
though they may also contain disturbing, thought-provoking,
or scientifically sophisticated elements. Wolfe's stories
are, in contrast, ambiguous in their implications and conclusions. They are lucid, yet mysterious and baroque, and
leave unprepared and unsophisticated readers baffled.

The atypical and challenging nature of Wolfe's fiction
partially explains his reputation in science fiction as a
writer better known to science-fiction writers, editors, and
critics than to science-fiction readers in general. Malcolm
Edwards' evaluation in The Science Fiction Encyclopedia
echoes an opinion often stated in editorial introductions to

8

Wolfe's anthologized stories: "greatly underrated, Gene Wolfe is one of the finest modern SF writers."(9) Wolfe has indeed been underrated, not in reviews but by the extent of his readership, as his performance in Nebula and Hugo award competitions demonstrates. Wolfe has appeared at least twenty times on the final ballot for the Nebula Award, which is voted upon by members of the Science Fiction Writers of America. His novella, "The Death of Dr. Island," won in 1973, and the second volume of The Book of the New Sun, The Sword of the Lictor, won in 1981. He has appeared only five times in the final ballot for the Hugo Award, voted upon by fans attending the yearly world science fiction convention. However, 1981 marked a change in Wolfe's popularity: three of his books appeared on the May, 1981, Locus science-fiction bestseller list--The Claw of the Conciliator in first place, The Shadow of the Torturer in third, and Gene Wolfe's Book of Days in eleventh. Charles Brown, the compiler, noted that this is a record.

Wolfe's concerns as a writer, and his style, indicate part of the reason for his slow rise to popularity. The rest of the reason stems from distribution. To be widely read, a science-fiction writer needs exposure--books on newsstands and stories in popular science-fiction magazines. Before The Book of the New Sun, Wolfe did not have that kind of exposure. Though Wolfe's science-fiction career began in 1966, with the publication of "The Dead Man," he had only two book-length science-fiction publications before 1980: Operation ARES (1970), which was usually out of print in the U.S., though more popular in England, and The Fifth Head of Cerberus (1972), which was more steadily available. Neither was a spectacular seller. Most of Wolfe's shorter fiction was published in book-length anthologies (especially Knight's Orbit series) rather than in the more widely distributed and widely-read science-fiction magazines. In 1980 and 1981, Wolfe's exposure increased. He had four book-length works published, all of which have appeared on the Locus best-seller list, including two short-story collections and two installments of his tetralogy, The Book of the New Sun. With the popularity of these volumes came reissues of The Fifth Head of Cerberus, Operation ARES, his mainstream novel Peace, and his young adult historical novel, The Devil in a Forest, advertised as a fantasy. During this same time period, four of Wolfe's mythologically-inspired science-fiction stories appeared in the widely distributed Isaac Asimov's Science Fiction Magazine. In 1982 and 1983, his stories began appearing in The Magazine of Fantasy and Science Fiction and Amazing Science Fiction Stories, and he completed his tetralogy. It

appears then that Gene Wolfe is in the process of becoming
not only a well respected but a widely-known science-fiction
writer.

This is as it should be, and Edwards' evaluation contains no exaggeration: Wolfe writes some of science-
fiction's finest prose. His prose has the complexity,
grace, and resonance to let it stand as superior writing
both within science fiction and within the wider world of
fiction. The Book of the New Sun may be his greatest
achievement thus far in a career that promises only to im-
prove. The expansiveness of its form and the literary ver-
satility of its hero-as-torturer beautifully suit Wolfe's
descriptive and symbolic power. A writer full of surprises
and delights, Wolfe offers the greatest of challenges and
rewards to those who study him.

NOTES

(1) Joan Gordon, "An Interview with Gene Wolfe," Science
     Fiction Review, Summer 1981, p. 18.
(2) "Gene Wolfe: An Interview," Vector, p. 7.
(3) Vector interview, p. 8.
(4) Gardner Dozois, "An Interview of Gene Wolfe," Xenolith
     One, p. 26.
(5) Vector interview, p. 13.
(6) Gordon interview, p. 19.
(7) Damon Knight, The Best of Damon Knight (Garden City,
     NY: Doubleday, 1976), pp. 9-17.
(8) Letter from Gene Wolfe to Joan Gordon, Sept. 14, 1978.
(9) Malcolm Edwards, "Wolfe, Gene," in The Science Fiction
     Encyclopedia, ed. Peter Nicholls (Garden City, NY:
     Doubleday, 1979), p. 660.

III

OPERATION ARES

Operation ARES (1970), Gene Wolfe's first published
novel, seems to have been written by someone else. Its
matter-of-fact prose, protagonist-as-mouthpiece, and concern
with political issues are uncharacteristic of Wolfe's manner, though some of his continuing interests do appear in
the novel. Wolfe shows his lasting concern with such issues
as ecology and the oppression of individuals by large social
institutions, but does so without his usual descriptive and
metaphorical language, his psychological exploration, and
his ambiguity.

Operation ARES posits a twenty-first century America
in which the welfare system runs rampant and a backlash has
slapped down the 1950's upsurge in government concern and
expenditure on science and technology. Instead, people distrust the sciences and fear individual enterprise. The
result is a repressed, depressed, and mechanically broken-
down society ripe for revolution. The novel's protagonist,
John Castle, finds himself part of a revolutionary organization called Operation ARES. Operation ARES is spearheaded
by invaders from Mars, people who had colonized the planet
when technology was king and were abandoned there when it
was dethroned. The plot traces Castle's involvement in the
Martian invasion and in the re-establishment of the ancien
regime, technological democracy. The novel's action is
divided into two sections: first, Castle's normal life in a
midwestern town under government control, and then his adventures after he leaves home--during his trek east as a
government prisoner, his sojourn in New York City, and his
involvement in armed rebellion.

The first part of the novel establishes Wolfe's
speculations about our possible future: a society under
repressive military control, one with its technology and
ecology in shambles, broken by such dangerous liberal
policies as an unwillingness to fight the Cold War and a
glorification of the welfare system--grim and conservative
speculations. Wolfe's technique is uncharacteristically
conservative as well, more reminiscent of vintage Heinlein
than of the more contemporary New Wave. The novel's
protagonist is an intelligent science teacher who serves
mainly as a mouthpiece for the novel's speculations and
philosophy. Such a role is an honorable one in old-
fashioned science fiction but unexpected in the work of an

11

author who usually avoids the techniques of the old school.

Wolfe supplies his protagonist with a relatively gratuitous love interest, in a gesture at humanizing the spokesman for his political concerns. The gesture is casual, the relationship undeveloped, and John Castle remains less convincing as a living being than even minor characters in most of Wolfe's other work. Exposition comes in undigested blocks rather than being absorbed in the natural course of story-telling. Wolfe introduces his speculations and ideas through tv broadcasts, Castle's lectures to his students, and political dialogues with his Nemesis, the Captain. Thus, such strained dialogues as the following deliver Wolfe's message.

> Almost bringing the fight into the open, John asked, "Why don't you make the raid tonight? You could, I know."
>
> The Captain chuckled. "I find my men do a more thorough job on barns and outbuildings by daylight, Mr. Castle."
>
> "Still amateurs after twenty years, Captain?" It had been that long since rioting had made possible the suspension of the Constitution and the installation of a President Pro Tem chosen from among the bureaucrats administering the welfare programs.
>
> "Now, Mr. Castle, that is just the sort of thinking that will get your name on a little slip like mine. When the old police were dissolved by the public will, our agency came into being to offer something better."
>
> "What you mean is that the people who put you in power wouldn't stand for a real police force so they got you—too weak to protect, but strong enough to oppress. If the armed forces hadn't been gutted at the end of the Cold War it could never have happened." (Ch. 1, p. 18-19, OA)

The first part of the exchange propels the story, but Wolfe's real concerns become evident too quickly. We learn through an awkwardly inserted bit of exposition--"It had been that long . . ."--several details of this future America Wolfe imagines. Castle's last speech shows the novel's political stance, portraying welfare as weak but oppressive and a strong military as necessary to societal well-being, without much concern for character-building. Such emphasis on politics over story is atypical of wolfe,

and the first section of the book makes clear that this is
blatantly a novel of ideas.

The second and larger portion of the book emphasizes
actions in the world built by the earlier exposition. It is
much more lively, subsuming exposition to action, and containing escapes, tactical maneuvers, battle sequences, and
night journeys through New York City. Wolfe's political
stance remains overt, expressed in stilted political discussions among the characters. However, daring escapes,
strange religious rituals involving lions, and dramatic ex-
plosions make this portion seem less heavy-handed.

One of the most fascinating scenes of this section is
Tia Marie's Hunting ritual in Chapter Six: it fascinates
largely because of its mysticism and mystery, qualities
generally absent from Operation ARES. "Tia Marie believed,
or pretended to believe, that the entire structure called
civilization was an illusion cast by man on mankind":
hence, her cult of the Hunters who shuck off the illusion
and follow such "uncivilized" practices as "astrology and
animism, spiritualism and the Seven Works" (Ch. 6, p. 95,
OA). For the benefit of followers and a visiting dignitary,
she stages a miracle consisting of the sudden appearance and
disappearance of a huge lion as the cultists chant for him
to bring them a successful hunt. The scene is dramatic and
stirring, but Wolfe purposely deflates its grandeur by ex-
posing the whole demonstration as a trick. The exposé
changes the scene from the shadowy ambiguity of Wolfe's
speculative fiction to the sharp-edged, thorough explanation
of traditional science fiction and indicates how different
the aims of Operation ARES are from those of most of Wolfe's
fiction. Typically, Gene Wolfe uses ideas and speculations
to build a work of literature; here he uses the medium of
literature to build his ideas and speculations. The concern
is not fiction writing but politics and the shift illustrates something about the nature of the novel of ideas.
The most noticeable stylistic discrepancies between Operation ARES and Wolfe's other work include its lack of
psychological probing, descriptive scene setting, metaphor,
word play, and ambiguity. These elements involve the reader
in the world of the novel rather than in its ideas and make
the search for meaning in the novel as important as the
meaning itself. A novel of ideas such as Operation ARES, on
the other hand, takes care to provide large signposts so as
to avoid the search, signposts such as conversations and
lectures devoted almost exclusively to the novel's ideas and
the repetition of key phrases.

In Operation ARES the key phrase is "power dwells in
the heart," which Wolfe goes on to explain through dialogue:

> "It was something my mother used to say.
> Usually it meant the city wouldn't fix the
> streets. . . . She always said it when she was
> talking about how much better ordinary people
> were than bigwigs. . . ."
>   "Because we are setting out to humble the
> powerful, in a sense." (Ch. 8, p. 137, OA)

Although the phrase suggests that the most powerful
defenders of a land or an idea are those whose convictions
are most heartfelt, Wolfe interprets it in a less predictable way (and that unpredictability is certainly typical of
the bulk of Wolfe's writing): power dwells, or should
dwell, within discrete individuals rather than in con-
glomerate power structures. Interpreted in this way, "power
dwells in the heart" summarizes the triumvirate of conservative political views which this novel espouses: rugged individualism, laissez faire economics, and isolationism.

The constitutional president, an old man named Hug-
gins, makes a speech to the people, attempting to persuade
the nation to reject the Pro Tem President and his government by cabal, while warning against the Pro Tem
Government's liberal and internationalist policies.

> We have no freedom now, though at least our
> tyrants are our countrymen, but we will lose
> that satisfaction together with our language and
> our heritage. As a people we have been
> entrapped by our desire that someone else do for
> us the things we should have done for ourselves.
> At first that someone else was to be our own
> government; then, when that government did not
> in our opinion do enough, we threw it down and
> put in its place that fraction of its employees
> who offered us the greatest bribe. If we wait
> now for someone else to restore our freedoms, we
> will wait for ever. (Ch. 9, p. 158, OA)

The speech warns modern readers about the dangers of our
contemporary government "by cabal" and is meant to apply not
only to what could happen in the twenty-first century but to
that which is happening now.

Through the demands John Castle makes for the restoration of the Constitution in the twenty-first century, Wolfe
makes specific recommendations for the restoration of Constitutional democracy he believes has been lost in the twentieth (or believed, at least, when he wrote the novel).

14

"We want the right to possess arms restored to
everyone except minors and those with a record
of narcotics addiction or criminal activity . .
. . We want a complete end to the system of welfare payments. . . . We intend . . . to set up—
by constitutional amendment, as a right—an ir-
revocable income for every citizen. . . . If we
. . . can hammer out a peace that leaves both
sides intact, both Russia and China will feel
that they still have a chance of gaining a position of paramount influence. . . . They'll bid
against each other, and with a little diplomacy
we should be able to keep the bidding running
for years." (Ch. 10, p. 203-206, OA)

Though the novel espouses traditional right-wing virtues,
its suggestions for achieving those virtues hardly follow
conservative party line—Wolfe's ideas are never completely
predictable. The recommendations, however, are so specific
that the novel's didactic purpose, to proselytize a clear-
cut social program, becomes clear enough that ambiguity and
an invitation to interpret have no place. So businesslike
is Wolfe in the attainment of his goal that he has little
time for the playfulness of language which usually distin-
guishes his work. He may make a pun, but he goes on to explain it:

"We don't any of us mind; set me straight."
Looking at him John wondered if he could be un-
conscious of the irony of what he said, for
Japhet was a hunchback. (Ch. 1, p. 8, OA)

Though Japhet may miss the pun, we don't. Wolfe may name
opposing generals Grant and Lee, but he goes no further in
suggesting parallels between the nineteenth century Civil
War and the twenty-first century one. Matters are not open
to interpretation.

In its straightforward confrontation of issues and its
relative lack of concern for literary techniques, then,
Wolfe's novel of ideas is atypical of his canon. Nevertheless, it deals with the two most common themes of his
sociological stories: ecology and the power of systems over
individuals. The ecological disaster of Operation ARES
stems from an overabundance of predators in the wild and a
depletion of fossil fuels; both imbalances develop because
of a lack of interest in pure science. Not only do
predatory animals escape from abandoned zoos to flourish

15

among their smaller and weaker cousins, but lack of scientific knowledge leads to the diminution of the qualities of civilization. until humankind returns to its more vulnerable condition of huddling around night fires to keep predators at bay. The steady supply of fossil fuels depends upon constant scientific exploration, as oil company publicity frequently points out; in the twenty-first century of Operation ARES, that and all scientific work have been almost completely abandoned. Science has been supplanted by a foolish but oppressive bureaucracy that traps individual citizens. However, this power structure has an advantage over those in most of Wolfe's sociological stories: it is well-defined. No one struggles to discover his or her role or stumbles through the bureaucratic maze. John Castle and his fellow rebels know exactly where they are lodged in the system and this knowledge enables them to break out and successfully revolt. The lack of confusion explains the novel's lack of ambiguity; the lines in Operation ARES are clearly drawn.

We can see why Wolfe chose to write his first published novel as he did, dealing with themes typical of his work in an atypical way so as to keep the novel's ideas always clear and present. But why did he choose to write this sort of novel when his previous and subsequent work is so different? There are two answers to the question which complement rather than exclude one another: first, Operation ARES may have been written much earlier than its 1970 copyright suggests and may therefore reflect a different stage in Wolfe's writing, before he had established for himself his characteristic manner; and second, the published novel may not be the story he originally wrote, and the alterations may also account for its atypical nature.

It seems sensible to suggest that Operation ARES does not have the watermark of Wolfe's distinctive style because it had been written before his self-confidence as a writer had developed thoroughly enough to produce such a style. Operation ARES, with its scientist protagonist, its plot of Martian invasion, its blocks of exposition, and its emphasis on ideas and speculations over literary technique, shares much with the genre science fiction of the 1950s: one can imagine the novel being successfully serialized in Analog Magazine. Its similarity to this conservative science fiction may be the result of Wolfe's beginning his science-fiction career by an apprenticeship of imitating already-successful practitioners. The result is clear, logical, and precise, three important virtues in the work of such conservative writers as Isaac Asimov, although the product of such virtues is not particularly subtle. In fact, subtlety marks

16

an experienced and confident writer more often that it does a novice. We may speculate that Wolfe began his career with the urge to express his views on politics and government policy in novel form, but without the confidence in his ability to convey those views through implication rather than direct statement; it is the compulsion of the novel's political views that weakens it. Political views do not age well, for the pressing concerns of one decade become the trivia of another, and Wolfe himself has changed his politics for more liberal views. A novel, therefore, cannot depend for long upon its political stance to remain vital. If a novel's raison d'etre is its political attitudes, then, the work fails to engage once readers lose interest in those views. Other work by Wolfe recognizes this vulnerability and translates politics into more lasting views on the human condition in general, expressed with more attention to the fiction that surrounds and incorporates these views.

A look at the publishing history of Operation ARES suggests other reasons for its atypicality. It began in 1965 as an unpublished short story consisting of what is now the first chapter. At Damon Knight's suggestion, Wolfe expanded it to novel length in 1966 and 1967. Though Don Benson at Berkley accepted the 100,000 word manuscript, he wanted it cut to 80,000 words. They fell to work, Wolfe cutting the first half of the novel by tightening sentences, Benson cutting the second half by excising entire paragraphs. The result of this expansion and contraction appeared in 1970, its manner no doubt changed by editorial circumstances. Expansion took away whatever enigma the first chapter offered about the chances for revolution or about the true power or even existence of a Martian colony. What was suggested or implied in Chapter One was eventually explained and elaborated upon, and this expansion may well have trampled the enigmatic quality that pervades most of Wolfe's fiction. The cutting of 20,000 words, as well, must have had a significant impact on the telling of the story. Much of what did not contribute directly to plot and theme would have disappeared--metaphor, description, meditation, elements which make up Wolfe's distinctive style--and with them disappeared any subtlety that might have been present in the original. Perhaps the 100,000-word version of Operation ARES would have contained more fictional accouterments and seemed less an aberration of Wolfe's corpus.

While Operation ARES is an aberration, it is not a monster. It is clear, straightforward, and moderately entertaining in its speculations, though it dares nothing artistically and offers no more than a routine contribution to old-fashioned, hard-core science fiction. The book was not widely or enthusiastically reviewed, but it does not invite condemnation. It is a journeyman effort by a man who later graduated to full guild membership, and it illustrates the difference between the production of a journeyman and that of a master.

IV

THE FIFTH HEAD OF CERBERUS

Until the success of The Book of the New Sun, The Fifth Head of Cerberus was Gene Wolfe's best-known work for several reasons besides quality. The cycle of three novellas is book-length and therefore more visible than single novellas or short stories in magazines and collections. The title novella, which first appeared in Damon Knight's Orbit 10, was nominated for the 1972 Nebula Award and the 1973 Hugo Award for best novella, and so it made a name for itself as an individual piece.(1) The cycle appeared in 1972, though its real success did not occur until 1976. In that year, Ace published the work in paperback, with a perceptive and flattering afterword by Pamela Sargent. Also in 1976, Neil Barron noted it in his bibliography Anatomy of Wonder, praising "the complexity, meaning, and sheer beauty of these excellently written stories."(2) The two events combined availability with admiration: since then, The Fifth Head of Cerberus has remained in print almost constantly.

Though the cycle consists of three novellas, Wolfe had not originally envisioned such a collection. In March, 1970, he sent the novella "Fifth Head of Cerberus" to Damon Knight as his Milford Conference story. Knight bought it for Orbit.

> Norbert Slepyan, who at that time was an editor at Charles Scribner's Sons, attended Milford, read "Fifth Head," and told me that if I would write two more novellas to go with it, they would publish the three as a book. I wrote "'A Story' by John V. Marsch" and sent it to him, and he sent me a contract. Then I wrote "V.R.T."(3)

Economics, apparently, can inspire art.

The three novellas share two common worlds, Sainte Croix and Sainte Anne; a common character, John V. Marsch; and common questions about the nature of humanity, identity, and memory. The first novella is a coming-of-age piece written from the first-person viewpoint of a young man known only as Number Five. Its setting is a French-settled city, Port-Mimizon, on Sainte Croix. The grotesque atmosphere is a cross between the fictions of Graham Greene and Mervyn Peake, and the plot revolves around Number Five's search for himself amidst a world of clones. The second novella, "'A Story,' by John V. Marsch," is a myth about the natives of Sainte Croix's sister planet, Sainte Anne, as it has been reconstructed by this minor character from the first novella. The myth's protagonist is a twin in a world of shape-changers and his story is a puzzle. "V.R.T.," the third novella, uses a collection of documents-- transcriptions of tapes, notebooks and diaries--to trace Marsch's anthropological tour among the shape-changers of Sainte Anne and his subsequent imprisonment on Sainte Croix.

The Fifth Head of Cerberus illustrates a number of representative traits in Wolfe's fiction. It forms a cycle of stories, as do his "Island of Dr. Death" trilogy (TIOD), the four "Thag" stories (Continuum 1, 2, 3, and 4), and the four-volume Book of the New Sun. It consists of novellas, a form in which Wolfe excels: other novellas of a similar calibre are "Tracking Song," Forlesen," and "Seven American Nights" (all in TIOD). It uses science-fiction models, such as aliens and clones, to explore thematic issues of identity and humanity, and it uses ambiguity and lack of resolution to express the complexity of those ambiguous and unresolvable themes.

Because it takes the form of a reminiscence looking back on a completed set of events and because its narrator is a human being, the title novella provides the clearest and most straightforward vision of life on the sister planets of the cycle. But the questions the narrator raises are exceedingly complex: "I seek self-knowledge. . . . We wish to discover why we fail, why others rise and change and we remain here" (Ch. 1, p. 72, FH). Number Five hopes that the act of writing will unlock his memory and answer his questions:

> I have written to disclose myself to myself, and I am writing now because I will, I know, sometimes read what I am writing and wonder.
> Perhaps by the time I do, I will have solved the mystery of myself; or perhaps I will no longer care to know the solution. (Ch. 1, p. 72, FH)

Though Number Five never discovers why his family stagnates and though, since the closing paragraph of the novella shows him repeating his father's history, he himself does not change. His story contains the answer.

Number Five, his brother, his aunt, his father, and his grandfather, as well as countless slaves in the marketplace, are clones of his great-grandfather, whose mind

20

is further replicated within the computer-tutor, Mr. Million. Tall, high-shouldered, and sharp-chinned, the clones form a single race that never progresses. Number Five has the same genetic composition as his father, is raised in identical surroundings, repeats his father's history, and believes that the course of drug-induced therapy that his father has forced upon him has resulted in "the destruction of my self," whatever kernel of individuality remains in a person whose nature and nurture replicate exactly his father's (Ch. 1, p. 62, FH). Nonetheless, Number Five's father is able to state that "we have our little variations" because "you don't know how difficult it is to prevent spontaneous differences" (Ch. 1, p. 66, FH). We realize that this stifling of differences causes the family's stagnation, though Number Five does not realize it when he confronts his father and Dr. Marsch in the climactic scene.

Number Five intends to kill his father after he finds out why his father practices such self-destructive replication. His father explains that it is to continue the search for the reason for his family's stagnation. "We end at this level!" his father cries:

> After how many generations? We do not achieve fame or the rule of even this miserable little colony planet. Something must be changed, but what? (Ch. 1, p. 67, FH)

The family stagnates because it has lost the ability or the will to change. Each generation duplicates the one before, allowing no alteration in nature or nurture, and denying, while destroying through drugs, the existence of a third human element, its individual essence or soul. Number Five almost realizes the answer when he thinks, as his father speaks, of a dream he once had in which he and his aunt are becalmed on his father's yacht.

> I realized that the ship, as my aunt had said, did not make headway or even roll, but remained heeled over, motionless. I looked back at her and she told me, "It doesn't move because he has fastened it in place until he finds out why it doesn't move." (Ch. 1, p. 40, FH)

Yet he does not realize that he has nearly found the explanation he seeks: such cyclic reasoning becalms the son as it does the father. The story ends with Number Five continuing to run his father's house of prostitution, his experiments, and his cloning of another generation of seekers.

21

We learn what Number Five does not: that identity is a matter not only of genes and environment, but of one's soul as well. To deny the soul is an act of evil appropriate to the address of Number Five's home, 666 Saltimbanque Street. A "saltimbanque" is a showman or a charlatan: the house of prostitution at 666 requires a showman and a deceiver to succeed, and the experimentation with human life that takes place there requires a more serious kind of trickster, one who meddles with the nature of humanity. "666," from The Book of Revelations, is the number of the beast, of the Anti-Christ, and indicates evil. The evil at 666 Saltimbanque consists of denying humanity by attempting to foil its "little variations" and to stifle the development of individual self-hood, either by creating beings which have human shape but bestial character—like the clones which Number Five sees being sold in the slave market—or by stifling the experiences and memories that develop an individual soul, as Number Five's father does to his son.

If humanity is purposely denied at 666 Saltimbanque Street, where does it reside? Number Five seems undeniably human, as we experience the events of the story through his reminiscences. He was a little boy who played, a young man who fell in love, and an adult who in anger overthrew his father. Yet as a clone his conception was monstrous, in a way, and its intent, to duplicate his father exactly, denied his individual existence. And what of those clones of the father who failed, such as the four-armed arachnid slave who shares Number Five's face? "They're not people, are they?" Phaedria asks as she walks past a roomful of slaves, "They're a kind of animal really."

> From my studies I was better informed, and I
> told her that they had been human as infants—in
> some cases even as children or older—and that
> they differed from normal people only as a
> result of surgery (some of it on their brains)
> and chemically induced alterations in their en-
> docrine systems. (Ch. 1, p. 52, FH)

They began as human beings but ended up as animals, and the difference seems to lie in brain and endocrine function.

Mr. Million is a computer that contains the mind of Number Five's great grandfather. Where the slaves have animal minds in human bodies, Mr. Million encloses a human mind in an inhuman body, and he seems more human than most other characters in the story. He has emotions and he teaches, a form of nurturing that encourages growth rather

22

than stagnation.

We learn, also, that humanity resides in memory. When his father robs Number Five of his memories, he steals some of the boy's humanity. (His memoir may be an attempt to restore or affirm his humanity by restoring his memory.) Mr. Million's memories give him his emotional depth, and part of the reason for the slaves' inhumanity is their existence only in the present without consciousness of the past. Humanity thus comprises certainly commonly shared experiences: a sense of individuality, qualities of mind and sexuality, emotion, and memory.

Memory is a recurring theme in Gene Wolfe's work, and here as well as in many of his stories—"Forlesen" (TIOD), "Many Mansions" (GWBD), Peace, and The Book of the New Sun, for example—he uses an architecture of memory. There is a mnemonic device in which one imagines a house as completely as possible and then associates each detail of it with an item from a body of knowledge. To imagine the house is to call up the body of knowledge; the house forms a metaphor for the information one wishes to retain. Houses also serve as metaphors for the mind ("I dwell in possibility/a fairer house than prose," says Emily Dickinson(4)). It should not be surprising, then, that Wolfe frequently describes houses that evoke memory and describe minds. 666 Saltimbanque, both a brothel and a laboratory, encloses sensuality and science. It is large enough that Number Five, who grew up in it, comes upon strange passages; his explorations, both physical and mental, lead to unexpected discoveries. This particular house suffers from a gothic decrepitude with its "flaking parapet" and "shutter of twisted iron," which, "on a planet that has been inhabited less than two hundred years, seems so absurdly old" (Ch. 1, pp. 3 and 37, FH). Number Five's mind—with its faulty memory, twisted reasoning, and recollection of youth from a great distance—seems the same. Oppressive as 666 Saltimbanque is, Number Five must return to it as the seat of his existence, the only place where he can write "to disclose myself to myself," though the house is, as we must suspect Number Five's mind to be, "in a very confused state." They must be, because, far from learning why his family never progresses, Number Five ends his memoir repeating his father's history.

666 Saltimbanque is the spirit of place on decrepit and stagnant Sainte Croix. A more mystical, natural, and primitive spirit of place pervades its sister planet, Sainte Anne. Rivers, groves of trees, and caverns, rather than architecture, inform "'A Story,' by John V. Marsch." Marsch appeared twice, briefly, in the first novella, as an anthropologist from Earth who wants to discuss with Dr.

Veil, Number Five's aunt, her "Veil's Hypothesis," that:

> supposes the abos [the natives of Sainte Anne]
> to have possessed the ability to mimic mankind
> perfectly. Veil thought that when the ships
> came from Earth the abos killed everyone and
> took their places, so they're not dead, we [the
> Earth people, the human beings] are. (Ch. 1, p.
> 23, FH)

John Marsch uses Veil's Hypothesis and his own field work on
Sainte Anne, described further in the third novella, to construct a myth of Sainte Anne's aborigines in the second
novella. The myth is the simulated artifact of a culture
whose existence has left little trace. Further, it deals
with twin boys, dreams, and shape-changers: confusion is an
integral part of the story. Who is who, who is human and
who is a non-human native, what is dream and what is
reality, what is truly Annese and what is Marsch's
fabrication? These questions make the story the most opaque
of the cycle. The questions are unanswerable and are meant
to raise deeper and more universally applicable questions.
Who is who? Initially, one needs to discover in what individuality consists. Are identical twins essentially the
same being in two bodies or are they two identical but individual persons? Do people who fit exactly into their culture have unique personalities as well, or do they derive
their individuality solely from their roles within the
tribe? If the latter is the case, is it more true in primitive cultures than in technological ones? In asking who is
human and who is not, one raises other questions as well:
of what does humanity consist and what is the human being's
responsibility to other species? Is a crime against
humanity a crime when perpetrated against another species?
Is inter-species hostility any more excusable than inter-
racial hostility?

When the line between dream and reality is unclear, as
it is in this novella and for its characters, one ponders
the nature of the two states. Dreams affect an individual's
actions, and some believe that they can predict future actions, but can dreams actually change actions in the waking
world? Can they ooze out into real time? Do dreams report
the events of a world that exists simultaneously with, but
separately from, the waking world, as the Australian
aborigines believe? Marsch, the anthropologist, observes
Sainte Anne. To what extent can we trust the observations
of another, whatever his credentials? The anthropologist
writes a story to explain Sainte Anne. Would scientific ob-

24

servation be more or less truthful than this artistic observation? How can a person from one culture ever really understand another culture? If Marsch turns into his aborigine guide because that guide is a shape-changer (and that possibility is suggested in the third novella), then, he may be practicing the ultimate and only act of cross-cultural understanding.

Wolfe's tendency to raise rather than answer questions, a tendency characteristic of his work but uncommon in science fiction, is one source of his evocative power. By setting us to ponder questions, he evokes the sense of wonder and wondering in us, beyond science-fiction's already powerful claim through imaginative speculation.

Though Wolfe says he knows little of Australian aborigine culture, the Annese culture invites comparison. The Annese are called abos, as the Australian aborigines are called in derision. Like the Australian aborigines, the Annese believe in a Dreamtime, a period both very long ago and present now in the dream world, which explains the world and affects it. For both the actual and the fictional aborigines, a magical and symbolic world explains and exists alongside the "real" mundane world of facts. The Australian aborigines maintain a stone-age culture in a country with factories, airplanes, and satellite-spotting stations. The Annese have a culture even more ancient. While Wolfe was planning this novella he had been

> wondering which came first, tools or people. If tools (which I believe is the currently accepted answer) then there was once a race of tool-using apes. If people . . .(5)

The Annese abos of John Marsch's story represent a culture without the capability to use tools, and we see them as intelligent but alien, primitive in a non-pejorative way. This modern assumption of anthropology is shown here through fiction. The technological gap between the Annese and the human colonists is wider than that between the Australians and the English colonists, for the Earth colonists of The Fifth Head of Cerberus have mastered space travel. However, the moral gap between natives and colonists is much smaller than the technological gap, as the third novella in the cycle shows us.

"V.R.T.," the third novella, consists of tape transcriptions and diary entries, out of chronological sequence, bound together by infrequent narrative intrusions. The diary entries are John Marsch's field notes as he and a boy who may be an aborigine travel through Sainte Anne look-

ing for evidence of its natives. (Since the Annese use no
tools, there is little evidence of their existence and what
there is is inconclusive.) The transcriptions record inter-
views between Marsch and the government officials who have
imprisoned him on suspicion of spying and the murder of Number Five's father. The narrative, which is set off by
italics and comprises only a small and widely dispersed part
of the novella, follows an officer of the Sainte Croix
prison as he spends a hot night sifting through the
notebooks and tapes that form the evidence in Marsch's case.
The narrative thread evokes the same decayed, sordid, and
steamy atmosphere of the first novella: the officer reacts
with casual violence to the night's interruptions—a slave,
a cat, a bird—and copulates with the slave girl while he
absent-mindedly sorts through the disorderly box of evidence
in Marsch's case. The evidence reveals that Marsch has come
to an attitude as indifferent as the officer's toward the
possibility of release from interminable imprisonment in an
underground maze.

The transcriptions and diaries lead us to believe that
Marsch's voice actually contains two consciousnesses—his
own and that of the boy, V.R. Trenchard. When the boy dies
half-way through his trip with Marsch, it seems that his
consciousness joins Marsch's. Or, V.R.T. has changed from
his own shape, which is now that of someone dead, to
Marsch's more viable one. Or Marsch, the dedicated
anthropologist, has taken on the consciousness of his subject in a kind of schizophrenia brought on by cultural
shock, isolation in the wilderness, and imprisonment. The
result of this joining is as strange and fragmented as the
form of the novella:

> At least half of me is animal. . . . I do not
> really speak out like others, but only make cer-
> tain sounds in my mouth—sounds enough like
> human speech to pass the Running Blood ears that
> hear me. . . .
> This cell is beneath the cathedral floor
> itself, and since they bury the dead in that
> floor, with their gravestones paving the aisles
> and pews, the graves are above me, and it may be
> my own that they are digging; there, once I am
> safely dead, they will say masses for me, the
> distinguished scientist from the mother world.
> It is an honor to be buried in the cathedral,
> but I would wish instead a certain dry cave high
> in one of the cliffs that overlook the river.
> (Ch. 3, pp. 219-220, FH)

Each consciousness intrudes upon the other in this monologue. The anthropologist's understanding of his subject has become—whether through study, madness, or shape-changing—not only empathy, but mimicry or actual absorption. He has become his subject.

John Marsch seeks to discover the true identity of the aboriginal race, asking first whether it exists at all, and then, if it does, whether it retains its original form. But his problem is insoluble if the aborigines can change shape. Rather than discovering a single truth about the aborigines, Marsch loses the truth of his own identity. His loss makes us wonder. Can a person adopt a new cultural identity by imitation? Can anyone have a personal identity if he loses his cultural one?

The questions these novellas raise, their purposeful ambiguity, show us how complicated the nature of identity is, but speculative fiction makes it possible to explore the complications in a concrete way. Wolfe uses speculative fiction to externalize the search for self. Finding one's self is usually a figure of speech, but the characters in The Fifth Head of Cerberus actually go searching for self in a concrete way, in a concrete physical environment. When we describe a person who adopts a new culture by saying he turns into a member of that culture, we don't mean it literally—but an actual physical transformation can take place in science fiction. The Fifth Head of Cerberus exploits science-fiction's potential to turn metaphors into actual events.

The Fifth Head of Cerberus is quite a different thing from Operation ARES. Where Operation ARES gave political answers to material problems, The Fifth Head of Cerberus explores questions raised by more abstract and universal problems. Where Wolfe used a flat, seemingly objective and straightforward style in Operation ARES, he has used not only several kinds of storytelling but several perspectives in The Fifth Head of Cerberus to relate its much less straightforward visions.

To get at his questions of identity and memory, humanity and culture, Wolfe tries first a formal narrative, second a reconstruction of a cultural artifact, and third a collection of documents. In historical and anthropological writing, the difficulty of writing truth (the actuality of events and cultures) has long been recognized, and those same three techniques have been employed to arrive at some kind of truth. Truth, if it can be told, may be held in an interface among the three kinds of storytelling.

Wolfe uses three perspectives to make his exploration as well. The first novella is a memoir, looking back on events which occurred in the historical past. "A Story ..." occurs in dreamtime, the time when myths and magic coincided with and gave structure to physical reality; the powers of dreamtime can be called up into the present by retelling the myths, for mythic past and mundane present exist simultaneously. In "V.R.T." there is the present moment of recorded conversations and the journalistic immediate past, occurring without resonance or reflection. Again, a true understanding of the worlds of The Fifth Head of Cerberus exists in the multiple perspectives of history, myth, and immediacy.

The second and third novellas of The Fifth Head of Cerberus may have been written as something of an afterthought, it is true. And it might be argued that the title novella, the original one, is the best of the three. Certainly, it is the clearest, partly because of its cloning metaphors work convincingly at both literal and metaphorical levels and partly because its evocation of place is the most vividly handled through Number Five's Proustian narration. However, the real strength of The Fifth Head of Cerberus lies not in the strength of each individual novella but in the way the three form a larger entity as a cycle. Three narrative styles, three perspectives, three stories form one multifaceted vision. They have many nodes of connection: they take place in the same solar system and the two worlds share political, anthropological, and sociological assumptions; certain images, such as the silver trumpet vine, reappear; and they deal with the same themes--humanity and humaneness, identity, and memory. They are also linked by some mysterious, perhaps meaningless but nevertheless intriguing repetitions that establish minor but compelling harmonies as one reads one story with the echo of the others still reverberating. The letter V is such a curiosity--Dr. Veil, V as the Roman numeral of 5, stories by Vernor Vinge in the Port-Mimizon library, John V. Marsch, V.R.T.

In these attentions to stylistic details, as well as in his handling of complex issues in complex ways and in the grace with which he introduces information about his new worlds, Wolfe shows that Fifth Head of Cerberus is the work of a mature and controlled artist. Five years passed between Operation ARES and "The Fifth Head of Cerberus"; during that time Gene Wolfe grew more skilled not only in writing but in recognizing the forms, themes, and motifs best suited to his particular talents. He worked extensively with short stories and novellas, examining themes of identity ("The Toy Theater," TIOD), memory ("Remembrance to Come," Orbit 6, ed. Knight), and humanity ("Eyebem," Orbit 7, ed. Knight); and using motifs such as the lonely boy

("The Island of Dr. Death and Other Stories," TIOD), shape-
changers ("The Changeling," GWBD), and architecture ("House
of Ancestors," IF, June 1968). All these studies came
together, powerfully, in The Fifth Head of Cerberus.

NOTES

(1) Orbit 10 (New York: Putnam, 1972).
(2) Neil Barron, "Gene Wolfe: The Fifth Head of Cer-
     berus," Anatomy of Wonder (New York: Bowker, 1976),
     p. 276.
(3) Letter from Gene Wolfe to Joan Gordon, Feb. 24, 1982.
(4) Emily Dickinson, "I Dwell in Possibility" (#657), The
     Complete Poems of Emily Dickinson, ed. Thomas H.
     Johnson (Boston: Little, Brown, 1951), p. 327.
(5) Letter from Gene Wolfe to Joan Gordon, Feb.24, 1982.

V

<u>PEACE</u>

In 1975, after publishing more than fifty short
stories in science-fiction magazines and anthologies, after
publishing two book-length works designated as science fiction, and after making a name for himself as a science-
fiction writer's science-fiction writer, Gene Wolfe produced
a mainstream novel. <u>Peace</u> did not make a big splash: it
did not go beyond its first hardback printing until 1982,
when it was reissued in paperback as Wolfe's popularity increased with <u>The Book of the New Sun</u>. It received only a
few modest reviews, though one was in the <u>New York Times
Book Review</u>. Nevertheless, <u>Peace</u> is a beautifully written
and artfully complex novel that shows there is little or no
difference between mainstream fiction and science fiction as
practiced by Gene Wolfe. <u>Peace</u> unites Wolfe's most common
themes of memory, isolation, and rejection with another
theme, the nature of time, which will become more and more
important in his later work. It joins them in the form of a
fictional memoir with embedded stories, a form which serves
as a character study of its narrator at the same time it explores the nature of fiction.

The novel traces the life of its narrator, Alden Dennis Weer, as he grows up and becomes an established citizen
of Cassionville, Ohio, a quiet Midwestern town. Set in the
past, set in a place which, though imaginary, seems to represent typical small-town America, <u>Peace</u> seems quite outside
the venue of science fiction; the decision to publish it as
mainstream fiction seems obvious and inevitable. The only
strangeness occurs in the embedded stories and in the oddness of Alden Dennis Weer's perceptions. But the same could
be said of "The Changeling," "Three Million Square Miles,"
and "The Island of Dr. Death and Other Stories," all published in science-fiction anthologies. We see then how ar-
bitrary, inconsistent, and unreliable the division between
mainstream and science fiction, or speculative fiction, can
be. Wolfe tried to break into the more critically-approved
and potentially more lucrative world of mainstream publishing with <u>Peace</u>, but for several years, at least, the
novel suffered the fate of most first novels. Though this
was not Wolfe's first novel, Harper and Row called <u>Peace</u>
such, and for the readership at which it aimed, it was.

We can assume that greed and the urge for fame were
not the only reasons for Wolfe's decision. A reason more

helpful to our understanding of Peace lies in the
flexibility that the mainstream label allows in interpreting
the narrator's situation. Wolfe keeps his narrator's
precise situation ambiguous. Perhaps the old man narrates;
if so, he is casting back in time, either literally, com-
municating with his younger selves, in which case this is
science fiction, or figuratively, through the alteration of
his memories, in which case it is not science fiction. Perhaps instead, the novel is narrated by the middle-aged Weer;
if this is so, either he knows his own future, in which case
the novel is science fiction, or he imagines his future, in
which case it is not. Nevertheless, whether Peace is
speculative fiction or not, it is fiction which invites
speculation.

The speculation which allows the most symbolic
resonance is that Peace is narrated by Weer as a middle-aged
man suffering some kind of mental breakdown caused by overwork and loneliness. His memoir is largely a response to
the Thematic Apperception Test (TAT) which his doctor
decides to administer when Weer visits Dr. Van Ness to ask
for advice on treatment of the stroke he will have in the
future. Detecting something amiss in Weer's question, the
doctor runs a series of psychological tests. In the TAT,
the doctor shows the patient a series of pictures and the
patient tells stories inspired by the pictures. The
patient's responses reveal his psychological state.

Each question Dr. Van Ness asks triggers a long and
detailed set of memories. He asks Weer his age, and the
story of Weer's fifth birthday follows. The doctor insis-
tently calls Weer back from his reverie, gives him advice
regarding his future stroke, and Weer falls into a reverie
again, beginning with the beautiful meditation on the
"simulated stag" and wending its way through the Christmas
after his fifth birthday and a story the maid Hannah had
told him. These first two reveries are relatively short,
each only a few pages long.

Then Dr. Van Ness introduces the TAT. "Turn over the
first card. Tell me who the people are and what they are
doing" (Ch. 1, p. 40, P). The mere suggestion elicits
seventy-three pages of Weer's memories: Chapter Two,
"Olivia." This section covers the first part of young
Weer's stay with his aunt, her three suitors, and two embedded stories. When the doctor finally manages to inter-
rupt, Chapter Three, "The Alchemist," begins. The doctor
takes this opportunity to warn Weer of the dangers of overwork and shows him the first TAT card, which pictures a
woman or adolescent boy handing something to someone else.
Weer's response begins with his aunt's Chinese Story,

31

evolves into another of his childhood birthday parties at which Julius Smart tells a story, and then goes on to tell Smart's story. Over forty pages later, Dr. Van Ness offers a second card, "a figure writes at a table, another peers over his shoulder," and Chapter Four, "Gold," is evoked into being (Ch. 4, p. 166, P). This chapter describes the book-forger Gold, as well as a childhood ghost story and another ghost story which Gold has written.

At the beginning of Chapter Five, "The President," the doctor calls a temporary halt to the test and Weer returns to his own office (both the one he uses as the president of the orange juice plant and its reproduction in the old man's house). Weer misses his next appointment with the doctor, at which Van Ness would have outlined his conclusions about Weer's mental state, and the novel ends. We must draw our own conclusions. Weer is suffering from overwork, guilt, loneliness, and a sense of lost opportunities. He has difficulty forming close relationships, especially with women. Obsessed by his past, he provides himself with a future that will isolate him from everything except his own memories.

This view of the novel's situation allows us to see it as the richly developed character study of a man who shares much with Gene Wolfe:

> Weer is a man very much like me—I don't mean
> that the same things have happened to me, but
> that we have similar souls.(1)

Like his character, Gene Wolfe was an only child:

> It's a wonderful and terrible thing—terrible
> because one ends up being the last of the tribe,
> the only one who remembers the customs and
> teachings of the now-sunken land of Home . . . .
> I am the only one left, the only thing left; if
> I had to, I could not prove it was not all a
> dream.(2)

Weer lives in isolation from his land of Home. Responsible for another child's death, the young Alden is isolated from much of his small town's society as well. Later, when he is eight or nine years old, his parents go to Europe, leaving him behind with his aunt. As he grows older, the adults who populated his youth die, their houses disappear, the town changes, and eventually he becomes the last of his tribe. His memories, altered by time, experience, and character, take on the flux and unreality of dreams.

Wolfe shares something else with Weer—the pressures

of a job in management. Wolfe was senior editor of <u>Plant</u>
<u>Engineering</u>, where he "edits, buys some twenty-five free-
lanced articles a year, and writes a major cover story every
few months."(3) The responsibility of this full-time
management position, combined with personal and artistic
responsibilities, must have weighed heavily at times, but
Wolfe can relieve some of the pressure through the practice
of his art. Wolfe does not permit such a release to Weer
who manages a plant that manufactures ersatz orange juice.
Isolated, lonely, and overworked, Weer imagines himself
unstuck in time, a bit like Billy Pilgrim of Kurt Vonnegut's
<u>Slaughterhouse Five</u>. Weer, in his forties, believes that he
is also living as an old man, sixty or more, paralyzed by a
stroke, and alone in a huge house furnished with rooms that
recreate his memories. The isolation in rooms of memory
(where he frequently becomes lost) and the malady that
cripples his ability to communicate are imagined physical
situations that symbolize Weer's mental condition.

Alden Dennis Weer wanders through the rooms of his
memories, either literally or figuratively, attempting to
lay the ghosts of his past by recalling it, just as the
stories he remembers use ghosts to combat the tellers' fears
of them. By grasping and shaping his memories, Weer hopes
to earn peace for himself, to come to terms with the death
of Bobby Black, with his love for his Aunt Olivia (olive
branches signify peace) and for Margaret Lorn, and to
discover:

> What went wrong? . . . When I recall my
> childhood, and forget (as I sometimes do) every-
> thing else, it is quite clear what my life was
> to become. I was intelligent and industrious;
> Margaret and I loved one another deeply. I
> would marry her, and enjoy a career that, if not
> brilliant, would at least be locally distin-
> guished. . . . None of this happened. (Ch. 4,
> pp. 215-216, P)

If his exploration of his memories could show him what went
wrong, he might find peace. But we never learn why his
career failed; why he never married Margaret, and Weer never
finds peace. His memoir ends unresolved, as lives, not
novels, do.

Though unresolved, Weer's memoir is not a formless
collection of material but an artfully molded construction
designed to clarify its narrator's character. The novel
collects Weer's most vital memories. In Chapter Four, the
old, sick Weer interrupts the story of Gold to say that:

> Some things are, if not more important, at least
> more immediate than others, and so I must tell
> you. . .that I am very ill. (Ch. 4, p. 194, P)

This gives us a clue to Weer's (and Wolfe's) selecting
process. We are not presented with a detailed chronological
history of Weer's life but with a collection of his life's
most emotionally powerful events: his tussle with Bobby,
which ends finally with the other boy's death; the time he
spends with his beautiful aunt and his witnessing of her
courtship; the first time he meets Margaret Lorn; a tour of
the orange-juice factory which he heads; and the stories he
hears all his life. The doctor's testing does its job,
evoking those events of Weer's life that reveal the core of
his emotional being: his guilt over another child's death,
his failed love relationships, his work, and his imagination.

In fact, a larger proportion of Weer's memoir is taken
up by the stories he has heard than by the events of his
life. This ratio suggest that Weer may fail in his exterior
life because he lives so much in his interior one. Furthermore, we are warned to question the veracity of the exterior
events of his life, as he relates them:

> It may be that the only reason childhood
> memories act on us so strongly is that being the
> most remote we possess, they are the worst
> remembered and so offer the least resistance to
> that process by which we mold them nearer and
> nearer to an ideal which is fundamentally artis-
> tic, or at least nonfactual. (Ch. 1, pp. 20-21,
> P)

Thus, we learn that while Weer may not be able to release
his pressures through artistic expression, his memoirs are
artistic, "or at least nonfactual," and that he is, to some
extent at least, like Gold the book forger, "an artist shaping the past instead of the future" (Ch. 4, p. 231, P).

Weer makes it obvious, then, that his memories are not
to be taken as reliable imitations of his life, that they
are instead products of his memory and imagination. Was he
truly responsible for Bobby Black's death, several years
after their wrestling match? Dr. Black, the boy's father,
seems without rancor when he examines young Den. Or was the
cause and effect relationship between the tussle and Bobby's
eventual death the product of the imagination of a sensitive
and lonely young boy looking for a reason why his parents

rejected him?

Weer also makes it obvious that the unreliability of his memoir is caused not only by the quirks of his psychology but by his conscious awareness that his memoir is an artistic (or at least nonfactual) production. Though he may have felt little control over his life as he lived it, he holds the artist's control over it as he writes. Rather than using his power to provide his life with a series of false happy endings, Weer instead uses his story's form to gain control: the novel's form, a memoir with embedded stories, distances the narrator from his material, thus protecting him from being hurt by it. Weer recollects the events of his life from quite a distance; the old man, according to the chronological view, remembers events no more recent than fifteen years in his past. The middle-aged Weer, in his mid-forties, describes himself as a man of at least sixty to his doctor. Though we may choose to interpret the book's actual situation as the recollections of a disturbed man of forty-five, the book's form is that of a memoir by the older man. In using this form, Weer distances himself in time from the events of his life to distance himself from their emotional immediacy, though occasionally, their immediacy bursts through when he "must tell you . . . that I am very ill."

The novel's embedded stories themselves give its narrator added control over his life. The stories might be seen first as ways of avoiding particularly disturbing memories and second as ways of disguising memories by translating them into metaphors for the actual events. Third, however, the stories are always framed, and the frames serve to distance Weer from their content—he is not responsible for their invention. Only the brief meditations, such as the one on the simulated stag, originate with Weer himself; the rest are recollections of other people's memories. Some are framed only twice: Weer reads the fairy tale in a book or hears the Chinese tale from his aunt. But some stories have gone through several narrators before we hear them: in response to a Thematic Apperception Test, the middle-aged Weer relates what he believes to be the elderly Weer's childhood memory of a story his housekeeper heard from an Irish maid named Kate. If a story alters each time it passes through another narrator, as in the children's whispered gossip game, then the stories Weer tells us travel under heavy disguise. At the same time as they reveal Weer's feelings of isolation through their repeated images of ghosts, walls, locked rooms, buried treasure, and islands, they also protect Weer from the causes of those feelings in the exterior events of his life. They are not, after all, Weer's stories at all, but Kate's or his aunt's or Gold's. In telling those tales, Weer can feel as if he has escaped from his burdensome past at the same time he has escaped into it.

But this discussion of the form of Peace treats it as if Alden Dennis Weer were the true author, when we know that Gene Rodman Wolfe actually wrote it. If we step outside the narrator's frame, we see that Peace tells us about the relationship between truth and fiction: it is a fiction about the nature of fiction. Every time Weer warns us about the unreliability of his memories, Wolfe tells us about the connection between reality and fiction. Weer says:

> It may be that some of these events I describe
> never occurred at all, but only should have, and
> that others had not the shades and flavors—for
> example, of jealousy or antiquity or shame—that
> I have later unconsciously chosen to give them.
> (Ch. 1, p. 21, P)

Whether events occurred as Weer describes them, whether their emotional colors were as Weer says, cannot be known by the reader. Indeed, the exact nature of an event can not be known by anyone, nor can any two people agree precisely on its emotional value.

The precision of Weer's record is not the point of his memoir, nor is the impression of a precise record, of "realism," the point of Wolfe's fiction. Weer's memoir is true not to events, but to Weer's character: the past becomes a Rorschach, or a Thematic Apperception Test, significant and real only in its revelation of character. Wolfe's novel does not attempt to operate as a slice of life, duplicating events as they might appear to an objective observer. Denying the possibility of such a phenomenon as objectivity, Wolfe creates a world as it might seem to one person and strives to make it true to that vision.

Wolfe's story, rather than Weer's, is a metafiction: a story about stories. Gold forges books, Weer shapes memories, and Wolfe fabricates stories. Every time one of the novel's characters tells a story, we are reminded of the novel's fictive nature. Whenever a character stops his story before the end, as Weer does with the fairy tale about the princess, we are simultaneously reminded that real life is full of uncompleted stories and that we are listening not to real life but to a story. Wolfe's metafiction is not sterile, having to do only with its artifice. It is a self-conscious artifact which, through its artificiality, tells us something of the truth about reality. Trapped within our

36

own minds, we can understand the world only as it is mediated by our minds and memories.

Wolfe is very interested in memory, how it alters and how it preserves. He explores its nature in almost all his major work (the only exceptions are short stories). Wolfe carries out his exploration in a manner that suggests a melange of Dickens, Proust, and Borges and uses heightened characterization, meditation, and embedded stories. These three techniques, when used in a life story such as Weer writes, preserve memories by altering them into something memorable rather than mundane. When used by Wolfe, they show us how we all preserve our memories by altering them so that everything we remember is transformed by the memory into fiction.

Weer remembers his aunt and her suitors not as ordinary folks but as a strange, beautiful, and aloof heroine with her worshipful swains, each of whom has something to commend him, only one an adequate hero. Den sees Olivia's courtship in the same terms as those of the fairy tale he reads. Of Dr. Peacock the archeologist it might be said, as the princess says of her first suitor, "his kisses had tasted too strongly of fresh-turned earth" (Ch. 2, p. 23, P). Like the princess' second suitor, James Macafee is a merchant. Stewart Blaine, with his servants and his financial wizardry, parallels the princess' third suitor, who arrives with a bodyguard of aerial spirits, whose "kingdom was too insubstantial for me" (Ch. 2, p. 64, P).

Olivia's fourth suitor, Julius Smart, comes armed with a strange tale whose characters are Dickensian in their amalgamation of compassion with grotesquery. To characterize people in these terms, altering them into heightened types, is true to the psychology of a child who witnesses the acts of adults through his inexperienced eyes; it is true of the adult who romanticizes his aunt and his past; and it is true to the act of memory. Memory shapes the past into stories as a mnemonic device. Julius Smart, Olivia's one successful suitor, has the power to remember his history as a story. That power wins him Olivia's hand, and along with his being "the first major change to take place within my memory," it makes him "the central character of this book" (Ch. 3, pp. 122 and 159, P). The power to transform the events of everyday life into fiction is Wolfe's power; fiction admits the transformation, whereas memory doesn't always.

In addition to heightened characterization, Peace contains several very beautifully written meditations, each triggered by a single event or object of intense nostalgic strength. The most beautiful, most extended, and wittiest

37

meditation is the one that begins as Weer, the old man, searches for his old simulated staghorn Boy Scout knife. First Weer/Wolfe imagines "a simulated stag, his horns held proudly as those of any elm-deer" who ranges a forest with "trees whose leaves are dying with the summer in every color, like bruises" (Ch. 1, p. 16, P). The word "bruises" triggers the next fantasy, of "races unborn, withheld from us," whose "wonderful richness of stereotypes" he imagines, finally returning, by way of likening the bravery of the russet brown race to that of the simulated stag, to the Boy Scout knife (Ch. 1, p. 16, P).

As in Proust's Remembrance of Things Past, each memory evokes a vast and detailed scene, but, as in Borges' Labyrinths, the memories move farther and farther into fantasy, though without losing sight of the original source. By turning mundane objects into the stuff of fantasy, Weer charges those objects with unforgettability, and Wolfe, through these associational meditations, shows the extent to which the mind veers from the memory of a reporter, through association, to the memory of a storyteller.

Storytellers form an important part of Alden Dennis Weer's life. He doesn't tell others any original stories—though he fabricates meditations which are almost stories and his responses to Dr. Van Ness become the story Peace—but he absorbs many, many stories. The novel contains at least thirteen embedded stories, ranging in their complete-ness from several quoted passages in an invented book (The Lusty Lawyer) to the long oral story told by Julius Smart that takes up thirty-nine of the 264 pages in the first edi-tion of Peace. The stories vary in other ways as well, their totality representing a cross-section of storytelling forms and conventions. Weer reads several stories and has several others read or told to him; he makes them up and dreams them. There are Irish, Chinese, Arabian, and Yemenite folk tales, ghost stories, and mysteries. Most are fantasies; some are told as true stories with fantastic elements; some are non-fantastic fictions. Many have no en-dings, foiling expectations. In the fairy tale, though the requisite three princes display their courage to the princess, she refuses all three and the story is interrupted before she marries. One of the Irish tales is interrupted in the middle of a fight between a Christian rat and a heathen cat—we never discover who wins.

Weer himself doesn't finish his story: how did the egg get in the barn, why didn't he marry Margaret Lorn, does Dr. Van Ness ever present his diagnosis to Weer? Weer's stories reflect, then, his own experience of life as am-biguous and full of unresolved mysteries. Further, since

38

stories reflect their tellers, they are a good way for Weer to capture, and remember, the complex characters of the people he meets. The stories often show unexpected propensities for the grotesque or frightening in otherwise bland or controlled people, such as Aunt Arabella with her ghostly newspaper article, Julius Smart with his ghostly Southern gothic story, and Gold with his ghostly Book That Binds the Dead. Finally, the plethora of stories reflects Weer's tendency to escape into fantasy rather than attempt to resolve the mysteries of his life; he escapes his reporter's memory by concentrating upon his storyteller's.

Wolfe, the storyteller, concentrates so on these densely layered, Borgesian stories to show us not only the character of Weer but also the character of fiction. Fiction changes memories into stories, but it retains its obligation to memory, by saying true things about it: that memories are altered by the memorializers, that they are not always complete, and that they can serve both to escape and confront, to disguise and reveal.

Whatever memory does to alter lives in retrospect, it also preserves them and gives them a kind of immortality. Weer, fearing a desolate future even more than he does his unfulfilled past, preserves his past in memory, memoir, and architecture. Through his memory, he and those he remembers will exist until he dies; through his memoir, his memories will exist as long as there is anyone to read the book; through his house of memories, the physicality of his memories will be preserved until the structure crumbles.

> When I designed the entranceway of this house, I
> tried to recreate the foyer of Blaine's—not its
> actuality in a tape-measure sense, but its ac-
> tuality as I remembered it; why should not my
> memory, which still exists, which still "lives
> and breathes and has its being," be less actual,
> less real, than a physical entity now demolished
> and irrecoverable? (Ch. 2, p. 83, P)

Recording actualities as he remembers them in his memoir, building them in wood and marble, Weer extends his life beyond his death and brings himself a few years closer to immortality. The length of the extension Weer gains on his life is in direct proportion to the skill with which he builds his memoir and his house. This is, of course, the same proportion by which any serious artist, such as Gene Wolfe, operates.

The construction of the past is a lonely job: it isolates the builder from present and future. Still, it is a

chosen isolation. Wolfe's recurring concern with the causes
and effects of isolation and rejection extends to their unchosen circumstances. Alden Dennis Weer--whose parents
leave him with an aunt while they tour Europe, who loves
that aunt while she treats him off-handedly, and who holds
himself responsible for the death of another child--feels
rejected by parents, relatives, and his town. The unchosen
circumstances of his childhood gradually turn him into a man
who chooses to reject any close relationship, to isolate
himself from parenthood, from love, and from any but the
most minimal dealings with his town.

Although particulars of Weer's life are the causes of
his particular kind of isolation, Wolfe believes that isolation is a universal and inevitable, as well as a particular,
condition. Its inevitability and universality are caused by
the infinite variability of human perceptions. Weer's
memories of events do not match the memories of anyone else:
his vision of the world matches no one else's. Each human
being is isolated from all others because of the uniqueness
of each one's perception. In Peace a shared vision is
impossible; the closest anyone can come to that kind of con-
tact is through the sharing of stories. However, since
Stewart Blaine and Weer argue over the nature of the locked
room in Julius Smart's story, even the facts of stories alter as they are received by various minds. The memoir that
Weer writes, and the house he builds, preserve only
"actuality as I remembered it," an actuality estranged from
any other person's notion.

Such multiplicity of perception isolates stories,
storytellers, and listeners, reminding us that Weer's public
manifestations of his memory in memoir and architecture can
transfer only a clouded vision. Thus, the relative immortality that those manifestations might earn for Weer's
memory is not of the real thing. The real thing, the past
as Weer holds it in his mind, will die with him. Wolfe con-
veys unreliability of "actuality in a tape-measuring sense"
by transmitting Weer's story through his clouded vision.
Just as Weer's narration is unreliable, then, so are the
novel's chronology and closures.

Because of the novel's non-chronological order, we
must cautiously and hesitantly piece together the order of
its events, and we cannot know the precise nature of its
narration: whether it is told by the old man disabled by a
stroke, by the middle-aged man suffering a mental breakdown,
or even as is suggested in Chapter Two, by the young boy
lying "sprawled beside my candle and tiny smoking dish,"
overcome by the fumes of his chemistry set (Ch. 2, p. 71,
P).

40

We cannot count on any sense of closure in this novel, either, though that sense is a great comfort in many novels. Weer/Wolfe never tells us how the story of the princess and her suitors or the story of St. Brandon ends. We never discover how the painted egg got in the barn or whether Aunt Arabella's ghost was real. Mysteries remain unsolved not only because they remain unsolved in real life, but because their lack of closure leaves us uncertain, hesitant, disoriented, isolated from tape-measure actuality even in the world of the novel, just as the lack of chronology does.

In Peace, techniques of unfinished stories and non-chronological order serve themes of isolation and rejection. They also serve the novel's science-fictional speculation about the nature of time. Surprisingly concrete among the novel's more abstract concerns, these briefly mentioned speculations seem out of place and significant only as an indication that the narrator is desperate to find a rational, "scientific" explanation for his disorientation, and worth noting only because they recur in "Seven American Nights" and The Book of the New Sun. Actually, however, the speculations have powerful thematic importance.

> Matter and energy cannot be destroyed, Doctor [it is the boy of four who speaks with uncharacteristic erudition]. Only transformed into one another. Thus whatever exists can be transformed but not destroyed; but existence is not limited to bits of metal and rays of light—vistas and personalities and even memories all exist. I am an elderly man now, Doctor, and there is no one to advise me. I have cast myself back because I need you. I have had a stroke. (Ch. 3, p. 174, P)

Reason tells us that no boy of four could have spoken these lines, that they actually arise from the unreliable memory of the older man. The very outlandishness of the speculation, especially in the mouth of a young child, emphasizes how unreliable that memory is. Yet, though the unreliability and variousness of memory seem to deny humanity the same immortality that memory seemed at first to allow us, this passage restores hope. Memories do, indeed, exist. "Whatever exists can be transformed but not destroyed." True, the law of physics applies to matter and energy, not to memory, but the idea that transformation does not mean destruction leads us to realize that the law, transferred to metaphysics, makes metaphorical sense. Preservation of memories, no matter how isolated, isolating, altered, or

41

various these memories might be, is possible, even though the memories saved are transformed from tape-measure actuality to remembered actuality. The transformation is nothing to cause despair. It is, after all, the artist's act to make the world more meaningful or poignant by transforming it in a significant way. Weer has done that for himself by writing his memoir. Wolfe has done it for us by writing *Peace*.

NOTES

(1) Joan Gordon, "An Interview with Gene Wolfe," *Science Fiction Review*, Summer 1981, p. 19.
(2) Gordon interview, p. 18.
(3) Michael Dirda, "Gene Wolfe Talks About 'The Book of the New Sun,'" *Washington Post Book World*, 30 Jan. 1983, p. 11.

VI

THE DEVIL IN A FOREST

The cover of the paperback edition of The Devil in a Forest (1977) does a curious thing. It misleads its potential readers into thinking that Gene Wolfe, the science-fiction writer, has written a fantasy. "A beautifully told fantasy," says the blurb. The back cover refers to "the endless struggle between Good and Evil," fantasy's central conflict, and lists the Barrow man, "the awesome spirit of a long-dead but still-worshipped warrior," as a main character. Actually, the Barrow Man appears only in a dream, the demarcation between good and evil is not tidily drawn, and nothing fantastic occurs in The Devil in a Forest. The novel is, instead, an adolescent novel, a historical novel, and a mystery that points out of the past into the future, toward The Book of the New Sun.

The Devil in a Forest (originally published in 1976) was inspired by the Christmas carol "Good King Wenceslas," as the brief passage "About the Author" at the end of the book tells us.

> I found myself wondering who indeed was that nameless peasant from whom most of us are, in one way or another, descended. ("About the Author," p. 223, DF)

"That nameless peasant" appears in the two verses from the carol quoted at the beginning of the novel.

> "Hither, page, and stand by me,
>   If thou know'st it telling;
> Yonder peasant, who is he?
>   Where and what his dwelling?"
>
> "Sire, he lives a good league hence,
>   Underneath the mountain,
> Close against the forest fence,
>   By Saint Agnes's fountain."
>   (p. 7, DF)

The good king does not appear except as "the man in the arm chair" in Chapter Twenty-two where, characteristically, he asks lots of questions (p. 212, DF). The peasant of the song becomes Mark, the adolescent protagonist of the novel,

who lives in medieval Europe, in the shadow of "the Mountain," near a royal forest and a Christian shrine called
Saint Agnes' Fountain. From this brief identification and
location comes Wolfe's story of the time when Christianity
and the old religion coexisted in Europe.

Out of Wolfe's decision that the protagonist would be
an adolescent came the novel's shape as an adolescent novel.
Typically, adolescent novels feature teen-age protagonists
with whom readers can identify; vocabulary, sentence structure, plot, and meaning must be straightforward without
being simple-minded to satisfy readers who are characteristically impatient yet mindful of their developing sophistication. More importantly, adolescent novels tend to
grapple with the kinds of moral dilemmas thrust upon teen-
agers specifically and human beings generally. The trick
here is to avoid pedantry and preaching. While adolescent
novels that fulfill these qualifications in a vivid and significant way are more difficult to write than they may appear, Wolfe succeeds without any suggestion of flatness or
triviality.

Mark is the major reason for the book's success as an
adolescent novel because he manages to be normal without
being mediocre. An orphan and therefore isolated as many of
Wolfe's boy characters are, Mark seems to have adjusted to
the condition of being without a family or a comfortable
life. As a medieval peasant, Mark's inadequate care—he's
always hungry and usually cold—does not set him apart from
others, and the typicality of his plight causes him to accept his estrangement and find ways to cope without seeing
himself as a martyr. His ability to cope, the ways he
scrounges for food, clothing, and adequate bedding,
delineate his character and make it interesting to people
who take the satisfaction of their basic needs for granted.
Modern readers recognize and share Mark's burgeoning
sexuality while they admire him for his use of reason in a
world where reason is rare. Normal and identifiable, Mark
is also admirable and exotic.

Wolfe adjusts his style to suit an adolescent audience
as well, and he does so without condescension. Arcane words
attract him: they lend mystery and strangeness to the mood
he so skillfully creates in his writing. Rather than give
up such vocabulary in The Devil in a Forest, Wolfe, who
knows that a medieval setting demands medieval details, uses
a few words with which a teen-ager might not be familiar,
but he tactfully explains them in the course of furthering
plot or developing character. In Chapter Fourteen, Wolfe
defines "dirk" and compares it to "misericorde" through the
voice of a professional soldier (p. 145, DF). In so doing,

44

he gives us insight into that character, whom Mark calls The Boar, and another, Sieur Ganelon, as well, by pairing the two men with their choices of knives.

Wolfe uses the typical rhythm and fluidity of his sentences to describe action and character rather than to draw setting, so often dreaded by teen-age readers. Describing the sudden death of the peddler in the novel's Prologue, Wolfe writes:

> It was as though he had been struck a blow and he never actually knew it was an arrow; but he saw his pack lying alongside him in the dust, and his own red blood on the road--and, for the moment, the peddler saw himself as a boy running with other boys in the streets of Prague.
> (Prologue, p. 12, DF)

The long sentence builds up a rhythm through its use of repetition, both of words ("and," "boy") and of sounds (lying, alongside). Wolfe also sets up a pattern of stresses, each unit of the sentence having six major stresses ("It was as though he had been struck a blow, and he never actually knew it was an arrow" or "and, for a moment, the peddler saw himself as a boy running with other boys in the streets of Prague"). Indeed, such emphasis upon number of stresses rather than upon number of syllables parallels early English poetry. This is a refinement that pleases literateurs without thrusting itself upon the attention of adolescent readers more interested in character and plot.

Another literary refinement that younger readers will also enjoy is Wolfe's use of balances and opposites that describe swiftly in a way both provocative and vivid. Describing Mark after a day with the highwayman Wat, Wolfe says:

> He was in that state of fatigue in which objects seem unnaturally sharp--as though swimming in clear syrup--and ideas invincibly evasive. (Ch. 8, p. 99, DF)

"Unnaturally sharp": that seems a familiar enough phrase, though its likeness to "swimming in clear syrup" is new; but "invincibly evasive," its balanced opposite, arrests us with its juxtaposition of finality with indefiniteness. Later Mark dreams of the Barrow Man clothed in crumbling chain mail: "the rings had turned to greenness in their decay, as herbs did in health" (Ch. 9, p. 104, DF). Mineral and vegetable decay and growth are compared in a succinct yet complex way through a sentence that balances opposites.

Wolfe develops characters swiftly and forthrightly, taking care to give even minor characters the complexity that will spark them with life. In Chapter One he devotes a full page to the description of Cope, the blacksmith, including Cope's physical appearance ("a belly not soft like Josellen's father's paunch, but hard as gristle"), his gestures ("pushing it [his hair] back with one hand"), his customs ("he was the most regular worshipper at St. Agnes' chapel"), his demeanor ("a childish sullenness"), and his impact upon Mark ("it sometimes seemed to Mark . . . that Cope shook the ground as he went home") (Ch. 1, p. 14, DF). Ever after Cope behaves consistently with this description, yet he surprises us as well. Wolfe sketches all the characters through similarly forthright description, consistent action, and plausible surprise, and, like Cope, they are all mixtures of good and evil.

The novel's plot also mixes good and evil. An outlaw, Wat murders innocents, yet he behaves gallantly and kindly toward many. This ambivalent character proposes an ambivalent bargain: he will cease robbing pilgrims on their way to St. Agnes' Fountain and thus bring prosperity back to the tiny village if the villagers will help him in one last robbery before he quits the region. The enacting of this plan, its complications and its aftermath, combined with elements of romance and implications of witchcraft, provide the story's plot. The combination of robbery and intrigue with romance and witchcraft would have strong appeal for adolescent readers.

The novel's plot does more than titillate, however; it is the vehicle for two lessons which Wolfe suggests rather than pronounces. Through Mark's experience with Wat, charming yet cruel, and the Abbé, reserved yet kind, he learns that it is unwise to follow thoughtlessly those people or notions most attractive or popular. Instead, he learns to rely upon his own reason to determine that which is good and to follow it, though good and evil are often intertwined. Neither Mark nor the reader is told about these lessons. The actions of the novel lead Mark to incorporate them in his behavior and the reader is led to agree with Mark's decisions.

By modern notions, the rationality of Mark's behavior might make him seem anachronistic, yet Wolfe works to present an accurate view of the early middle ages. That this science-fiction writer would write a work of historical fiction is not surprising. Both science fiction and historical fiction require the writer to create a foreign setting that is both convincing and accurate to the extent that research can make it. As great a leap of the imagination is required to create a world from which most of our technology is absent as is required to create one where our present level of technology is obsolete. How did people handle food preservation, clothing manufacture, communication, and security before refrigeration, sewing machines, printing presses, and burglar alarms? Wolfe shows how medieval peasants lived their normal lives having never even dreamed of the technology we now take for granted. Like the science-fiction writer, he does so in the course of normal story-telling rather than through long passages of explanation, as a history or science writer might do.

Wolfe incorporates his research about medieval life in the situations of the characters whose stories he invents. We learn how and where the innkeeper stores his food in the course of his serving meals to the townspeople, to Wat, and later, to Sieur Ganelon and his men. Mark is an apprentice to a weaver, and later Josellen makes him a coat: thus, we learn about clothing manufacture. The prologue shows us that a peddler served as the medieval newspaper, orally reporting the news as he moved from place to place. The militia that Mark's fellow villagers form is their only, inadequate, security against robbers.

These homely details evoke a picture of life lived on the edge of survival, yet lived with great satisfaction derived from each successful and ordinary triumph. It is a life made busy not only by everyday concerns and periodic troubles, but by the fact that it is lived during a time when pagan and Christian religions coexisted. The nature of their coexistence is Wolfe's major historical concern.

We think of the medieval world as one dominated by Roman Catholicism, represented, perhaps, by Henry Adams' celebration of the Virgin. But despite later idealizations, medieval Christianity still contended with the old nature religions, and the mainstream of Catholic dominance did not flow with the overwhelming force into the backwaters of country life. Mark's village is deep in the backwaters, close against the forest fence, and people have not completely abandoned the old ways there.

Mother Cloot and Wat represent the old religion, while the Abbe and Wat's alter ego, Sieur Ganelon, represent the new, with Mark hovering between the two forces deciding which way is his. Mother Cloot believes in the forces of magic and believes herself to be a witch, though she may be merely insane or addicted to drugs. She appeals to selfish primal instincts in her manipulations: to greed, sex, vengeance, and the impulse to preserve one's self. Wat, the outlaw, shows that her world view is shared by a young, vigorous, and charismatic man: it is not simply the view of a crazy old woman.

The Abbé is the logical representative of the new religion of compassion and reason since he is its representative for the community by St. Agnes' Fountain. The Abbé's stand does not have the impulsive appeal of Mother Cloot's, but its fairness and kindness attract the confused adolescent boy. Sieur Ganelon, the man of law (whose other side is Wat the outlaw), illustrates the hard cruelty of the new reason when it is divorced from compassion.

Wolfe makes clear his belief that the new religion of reason and compassion is the force of good and that Mother Cloot and Wat have much of evil in them, but he does not clarify the sides of good and evil until we have lived with the characters awhile. At first the Abbé seems quite a sinister figure, cold and aloof, Mother Cloot a feeble old woman condemned by superstition, and Wat a Robin Hood. Gradually we learn that, while these first impressions have truth in them, they do not help us determine where good and evil lie. Pity and charismatic attraction do not lead us inevitably to good, a tricky lesson that Mark eventually learns. Further, Wolfe shows that evil people may also deserve pity or be unjustly condemned, as Mother Cloot is, and that evil people may sometimes do good, as Wat does in helping the forest people. The evil of these characters lies in the impetus of their actions, impulse and instinct, and in the focus of their concerns, which is purely selfish.

Wolfe's historical novel places the battle between good and evil on the ground where Christianity and the old nature religions coexisted in medieval Europe. On this ground the Christian shrine of St. Agnes' Fountain stands near the pagan shrine Miles Cross. The Christian blacksmith, Cope, reminds us, in his strength and mythic size, of the pagan spirit, the Barrow Man. Mark's village lies on the border between the cultivated farmlands of the Christian folk and the forests where the pagan charcoal burners live. Mark and Josellen live where the old and new confront one another both geographically and philosophically, and part of their growing up consists of growing from the immature impulsiveness and selfishness of the old religion, as it is represented here, to the more mature reason and kindness of Christianity.

Not only does the use of reason catalyze The Devil in a Forest as a historical novel but it drives its action as a mystery novel as well. The Devil in a Forest is something of a Father Brown mystery in medieval garb. Wolfe sets up several mysteries: Wat's true identity and the nature of his final robbery scheme, and the location of Josellen's hiding place. The mystery novel form requires the use of reason, of course, by which the detective sorts clues and induces solutions. As in the Father Brown mysteries, however, reason moves at a deeper level as well. Through reason, good defeats evil. The Devil in a Forest shares this use of the mystery novel to probe the deeper mysteries of the nature of good and evil. In "The Blue Cross," Father Brown says:

> Reason is always reasonable. . . . I know that
> people charge the Church with lowering reason,
> but it is just the other way. Alone on earth,
> the Church makes reason really supreme. Alone
> on earth, the Church affirms that God himself is
> bound by reason.(1)

That which is truly reasonable is good and that which denies reason is evil. Thus does Father Brown uncover the criminal. Thus does Mark decipher Wat's true nature and motives, and thus does he find and rescue the woman whom he loves. He learns to use reason from the Abbe, the representative of the Church, and reason teaches him to trust both the Abbé and the Church. Reason solves both the lesser and the greater mysteries.

The path reason takes to come to reasonable conclusions, though not blatantly obvious, is more clearly marked than in Wolfe's adult fiction, more so especially than the path Severian follows in The Book of the New Sun. Nevertheless, the adolescent novel and the complex tetralogy share some basic characteristics, as if The Devil in a Forest were a trial run for the more complex work. One can draw parallels between the two books in their protagonists, their settings, and their thematic concerns with faith and reason.

Mark and Severian are in similar positions: both are orphans apprenticed to trades, Mark to a weaver and Severian to the torturers' guild. Each copes well with his situation though the world in which he lives is difficult and dangerous. Each is drawn to an outlaw, Mark to Wat and Severian to Vodalus, and each puzzles over the outlaw's, and his own, moral nature. Mark and Severian comprise a particular type of Wolfe's isolated child: orphaned, vulnerable because of the harsh world in which he lives, yet making a sane adjustment to his condition, each a survivor with a developing moral sense.

Though Mark's world lies in our past and Severian's in our distant future and Mark's lies somewhere in Europe while Severian's is somewhere in South America, in some important ways they do not lie very far apart. Each lives in a highly stratified society, divided into castes, structured into guilds with a wide gulf between rich and poor, educated and uneducated. Though Severian's world contains technology of immense sophistication, that technology is unavailable to most people, and their society, like Mark's, is a labor-intensive operation. Mark's medieval world is almost as strange to us as Severian's future one. Once Wolfe had found he could convey the special peculiarity of medieval Europe, he might have felt more confident of conveying Severian's Urth, which is built upon a foundation similar to medieval Europe though the final architecture is quite different.

The Devil in a Forest and The Book of the New Sun share similar foundations of a different sort: a belief in the connection between faith and reason. Mark and Severian find that every seemingly supernatural event with which they are confronted has some rational explanation. This does not destroy their faith, but strengthens it as each moves farther from belief in superstition and its attendant cruelty to belief in reason and its attendant kindness. For Mark the movement is from the old nature religions to Catholicism, and for Severian it is a journey from the old Urth through which he travels to the New Sun of which the Pelerines teach.

The Devil in a Forest prefigures much of the world and the world view of Wolfe's later tetralogy, but it does not have the complexity and richness of The Book of the New Sun. The Devil in a Forest is, for Wolfe, a simple book, appropriately for its projected audience. It is not, however, a simplistic one, nor is it crudely fashioned in any way. Rather, the appearance of simplicity proceeds from Wolfe's thorough control: his machinations are skillfully incorporated into the story without the roughness or abruptness of his first novel, Operation ARES. The Devil in a Forest is a deliberately modest novel by a master, not the unconsciously innocent work of an apprentice.

NOTE

(1) G.K. Chesterton, "The Blue Cross," in The Amazing Adventures of Father Brown (New York: Dell, 1958), p. 20.

VII

SHORT WORKS

Short stories and novellas form a large and exciting portion of Gene Wolfe's work. One, "The Death of Doctor Island," received the Nebula Award; many others, among them "The Island of Doctor Death and Other Stories," "The Fifth Head of Cerberus," "The Eyeflash Miracles," and "Seven American Nights," have been nominated for Hugos and Nebulas. Wolfe's stories more commonly make their first appearances in anthologies rather than in magazines, though short stories have appeared fairly frequently in magazines since 1979. Two collections form a sampler of Wolfe's short work for readers who wish to follow his skillful and delicate manipulation of these demanding literary forms. The Island of Doctor Death and Other Stories and Other Stories (TIOD), which was published as an original paperback by Pocket in 1980, contains Wolfe's most important novellas after "The Fifth Head of Cerberus": "The Island of Doctor Death" trilogy, "Tracking Song," "The Eyeflash Miracles," and "Seven American Nights." It also includes several of his best short stories: "Alien Stones," "The Hero as Werwolf" ("Werwolf" is Wolfe's personalized spelling), "Feather Tigers," and "Toy Theater." Gene Wolfe's Book of Days (GWBD), a 1981 Doubleday hardback, is a more whimsical collection, with its stories arranged according to their appropriateness to specific holidays. It includes fewer major stories than TIOD and more humorous ones: among its prizes are "The Adopted Father" (for Father's Day, naturally), "Forlesen" (Labor Day), "The Changeling" (Homecoming Day), and "Many Mansions" (Halloween). Wolfe's most important uncollected stories include "Remembrance to Come" (Damon Knight's Orbit Six); "Westwind" (IF, August 1973); his "Thag" series, which includes "Dark of the June," "The Death of Hyle," "From the Notebook of Dr. Stein," and "Thag" (Roger Elwood's Continuum 1, 2, 3, and 4); "The Detective of Dreams" (Kirby McCauley's Dark Forces); and "The Last Thrilling Wonder Story" (Isaac Asimov's Science Fiction Magazine, June 1982).

The more than eighty-five works represent a wide range of Gene Wolfe's techniques and concerns. To give a notion of their variety, I shall discuss them in a variety of ways. Chapter One formulated three categories for Wolfe's fiction: entertainments, sociological stories, and psychological stories; several stories will be examined according to their relationships to these categories. Wolfe often twists conventional science-fiction and fantasy expectations to surprise us, and I will discuss several other stories in terms of their manipulation of conventional expectations. The evocative motif of the isolated child recurs in Wolfe's fiction, and I will explore its travels and transformations. Two major thematic concerns recur in Wolfe's stories as well--the nature of humanity and the demarcation of reality--and these, too, will be explored.

Gene Wolfe's entertainments are his most accessible, because least demanding, stories: least demanding for his readers, that is. When Wolfe sets out to entertain, he offers the amusement of a clever and baroque game, and the story's construction demands a great deal of skill. "How I Lost the Second World War and Helped Turn Back the German Invasion" (GWBD), hereafter known as "How," represents the typical Wolfe entertainment, though it is longer than most (fourteen pages in GWBD). The story is filled with word play: "toy autos" for Toyotas, People's Car for Volkswagen, and race master for master race. The Toyota pun triggers part of the plot, the English translation of Volkswagen delays our realization of its significance, and the reversal of "master race" defuses the ugliest side of World War II in a way that reflects the function of the story as a whole. Numerous historical allusions to the World Wars form a series of punchlines, and the story ends without any feeling of ambiguity--we do not doubt the outcome of "Dwight's" final war game.

Entertaining as the word play, in-jokes of history, and punchlines are, they do not form a simple entertainment, but a very complex one. "How" is an alternate world story that answers two "what-if" questions: what if World War II had been fought economically rather than militarily and what if Hitler's madness had been benign rather than malignant: but "How" incorporates another story as well--the story of World War II as nothing more than a war game. The "what-if" story and the war game story are told as a letter to the editor of a strategic game magazine by a non-military Dwight D. Eisenhower. The "what-if" story triggers a race between British cars, Centurians, and the German People's Cars, with Japanese toy autos providing interference--that race forms an economic war game to parallel the military war game which Ike plays simultaneously. The race "forecasts" the United States' present economic relationship with Germany and Japan while the military game duplicates the tactical actualities of World War II. The story is as frenetic in its juggling of plots and parallels as the little cars which dodge around one another during the race.

52

As lighthearted as the gaming atmosphere is, as giddy as the story's maneuvering makes us, it has something serious embedded in it. Not only does the fictional Winston Churchill pronounce a wise pair of epigrams—"dishonesty . . . consists in violating rules to which one has . . . agreed. I simply proposed rules I felt would be advantageous, which is diplomacy"--but "Unknown Soldier," as the fictional Eisenhower signs himself, offers Wolfe's warning about our own future (p. 74, GWBD). Ike and his friend are about to begin a new game of "World War" with the United States, Britain, and China opposing the U.S.S.R., Poland, Romania, and several other Eastern European nations. There is every danger that the world map, which forms the game board, will be destroyed by coals from the players' pipes, just as two Japanese cities had been burnt off the map in their first game.

"How" conforms closely but not exclusively to the typical characteristics of an entertainment: it contains traits of Wolfe's sociological and psychological fiction as well. The embedded warnings about economics, war, and nuclear destruction remind us of Wolfe's sociological concerns. Reality and fantasy weave in and out as they do in the psychological stories, though the demarcation is clearer here to both readers and characters than it is in Wolfe's more psychological fiction. In the alternate world "How" presupposes, make-believe--the war game--mimics the world we know, while the economic war which is the 1938 "reality" of the story suggests our own contemporary reality (the story was written in 1973 and the hold Japanese cars have on the market has not significantly changed since then). Though "How" is a game, an entertainment, it makes serious points in a sophisticated way.

While "How" is concerned with economics and warfare, Wolfe's sociological stories more frequently warn us of the subjugation of individuals by organizations ("Many Mansions," in GWBD), the implications of technology ("The Woman Who Loved the Centaur Pholus"(1)), and the dangers which threaten the world's ecological system. "Three Million Square Miles," "An Article About Hunting," and "Beautyland" (all in GWBD) explore the consequences of destroying wilderness.

"Beautyland" is a short and sordid tale that shows in just five pages what becomes of people who care nothing for preservation of wilderness. Wolfe evokes rather than describes a future with harsh clarity--an America without parkland, every inch developed. The sociological warning of "Beautyland" is so fundamental to the story that every element points to it. No games or ambiguities dilute its intensity, and its artistry is that of clarity, purpose and vividness. The story, primarily a dialogue between two men, describes a world in which the urge to destroy is much stronger than any urge to preserve. This world of land developers, oil company magnates, entrepreneurs, defrauders, and potential suicides is presented as a direct extension of our own. The America of "Beautyland" has become the way it is because of callous indifference and greed, but that isn't the real wallop of the story. Many have warned us of the dangers of indifference and greed. For Wolfe, such sins are the givens of the story: he is more interested in the effects of a world without wilderness upon the people who live in it than he is in its causes. Given a choice between saving the last bit of wilderness and destroying it, Wolfe shows people so debased by their barren environments that they choose overwhelmingly and enthusiastically to destroy it.

Wolfe illustrates this horrible psychic result of ecological irresponsibility with a confession made by a rich man to the narrator, who is poor. The narrator chooses to call the rich man Dives, after the rich man of Jesus' parable in the Book of Luke. The narrator's use of a symbolic name, the confessional mode, the contrast between Dives' anguished contrition (he gained his wealth by capitalizing upon people's urge to destroy the last wilderness), and the narrator's selfish indifference to morality all drive the story's lesson home: wilderness serves the soul as well as the ecosystem.

When Wolfe's primary concern is to make a social statement, as it is in "Beautyland," he comes closest to using science-fiction conventions in a straightforward manner: here, the future as an ecological wasteland (see Chelsea Quinn Yarbro's False Dawn, Kate Wilhelm's Juniper Time, John Brunner's The Sheep Look Up). When his concern turns inward to the human mind, though he still expresses social concern, the worlds he describes have more of dream and less of probability to them. Wolfe's psychological fiction, full of mystery and dream, often addresses the difficulties of an individual in coping with large organizations: big business, government, society. This particular sociological concern turns back upon the individual and appears repeatedly in Wolfe's psychological fiction, from early stories such as "House of Ancestors"(2) and "The HORARS of War(3) through "The Island of Doctor Death" trilogy to his most recent work, The Book of the New Sun.

"Forlesen" (GWBD), an evocative, dream-like, and mysterious novella, is a psychological story with just such a

54

sociological thrust. "Forlesen" makes its warning about the subjugation of the individual within an organization by showing us a metaphorically universal situation, although actually strange and fantastic. The story haunts the mind rather than shakes a finger in the face, and by its dream-like atmosphere makes Wolfe's admonition seem more like premonition, evoking a feeling difficult to shove aside. Such is the power of the psychological story, because it explores the archetypal universality of a social situation.

Gene Wolfe has chosen "Forlesen" to represent Labor Day in his Book of Days because its protagonist is representative worker in a representative bureaucratic maze. His position symbolizes the way many people view their working lives. Forlesen wakes up to find himself in pointless employment as an executive in a plant. His duties are couched in meaningless generalities ("assist in carrying out corporate goals," p. 106, GWBD), and his time is spent in playing power games. What makes the story speculative fiction with Gene Wolfe's stamp is that its metaphors are carried to extremes and are described as actualities. Emmanuel Forlesen's (surely an emblematic name) typical work day is his only work day, and it covers a bureaucrat's entire career from his entry in the morning as a junior executive learning the ropes (and the sports cliches experienced executives use) to his late-afternoon retirement party. The story compresses a twentieth-century corporate career into a single day. In a life spent at meaningless work that deals in generalities and in getting ahead rather than in actual production, in a life that divorces one from one's family and individual needs, one day does indeed fade into the next so that one finds life over without ever having felt or done anything. Forlesen's world, like the world of Kafka's bureaucrats, is filled with pointless regulations that force the individual, for mysterious and no doubt pointless motives, into a pointless life. In this world Forlesen wanders in confusion, trying to catch on to the "game plan," ending his day, his life, without learning what possible purpose his life could have had. Taken literally, the situation is surreal. Taken symbolically, it is mundane.

Forlesen gains some small success in his corporation, vaguely named "Model Pattern Products," because he doesn't quite fit in. He is capable of original thought, evidenced by the way he analyzes a "Sample Leadership Problem." Rather than taking the problem at face value, he tries to learn more information about it to solve it wisely instead of merely correctly, with the result that another executive asks him for advice. Forlesen's glimmer of creativity, of non-conformist behavior, also makes him visit his family at lunch--a small effort at family life--and makes him examine the road on his way to work, attempting to learn something about his environment. Such creativity doesn't save him from a pointless career and an insignificant end, but it gives him a certain depth of character. In the world of "Forlesen," and perhaps in contemporary corporate life, this is all one can ask.

One cannot, it seems, ask for any certain answers. Forlesen finds none:

> "Everyone's entitled to an Explainer--in whatever form he chooses--at the end of his Life. He . . . may be a novelist, aged loremaster, National Hero, warlock, or actor. . . . Or a theologian, philosopher, priest, or doctor."
>
> "I want to know if it's meant anything," Forlesen said. "If what I suffered--if it's been worth it."
>
> "No," the little man said. "Yes. No. Yes. Yes. No. Yes. Yes. Maybe." (p. 128, GWBD)

The reader finds no answers, either. Forlesen cannot understand fully the situation in which he finds himself, nor can we. In the second paragraph of the story, we learn that "at the time he woke he knew only his own name; the rest came later and is therefore suspect" (p. 85, GWBD). This warns us that the remainder of the story, colored by Forlesen's perceptions, shows those perceptions much more reliably than it shows any information about his world. The novella's concerns are psychological, and its perspective is upon the interior life.

A few pages later Forlesen reads from a book meant to "tell you how to be good, and how to live--everything like that" (p. 89, GWBD). The excerpt Forlesen reads implies that the strange world into which he awakes is some form of afterlife. But the excerpt offers so many choices that neither he nor we are much wiser.

> Of the nature of death and the Dead we may enumerate twelve kinds. First there are those who become new gods, for whom new universes are born. . . . Fifth those who dwell in gardens of bliss, or are tortured. Sixth those who continue as in life. . . . Eighth those who find in their graves their mother's wombs and in one life circle forever. . . . Tenth those born

56

again as men in their grandsons' time. . . . (p.
90, GWBD)

Perhaps Forlesen is caught in the tortures of hell, or is
continuing as in life, or is repeating it, or is thrust be-
wildered into the future. Or perhaps not. The sociological
warning is clear--the dehumanization by corporate life--but
the metaphor that carries the warning is ambiguous, and the
ambiguity makes the warning more powerful. "Forlesen" makes
its sociological points, as well as its psychological ones,
by showing us the truth of dreams.

To illustrate corporate life with a Book of the Dead
is an unexpected twist. Wolfe makes frequent use of a different sort of twist. He wrenches our expectations of
science fiction and fantasy conventions. The title "The
Hero as Werwolf" (TIOD) indicates one such inversion: here,
of the traditional role of the werewolf in fantasy. The
werewolf is the protagonist, rather than the antagonist, but
that is only the first twist. Wolfe posits a future in
which Earth has been taken over by an alien race that trans-
forms most human beings into its own alien physiology.
Those human beings who remain human find all their food supplies usurped by the alien masters. To survive, the human
beings stalk, kill, and eat their masters, though the differences between the two sentient species seem slight. The
human beings, rather than the aliens, are the monsters in
their practice of a form of cannibalism, and the reader is
left in the strange position of empathizing with the practitioners of a monstrous act.

"Three Fingers" (TIOD) begins with a surprising view
of Walt Disney Studios as an evil Mickey Mafia and ends with
an unveiling scene which further confounds our expectations.
Michael identifies the three Disney characters who are
threatening him according to the archetypes which they
represent: Captain Hook is all the menacing sea captains
and pirates of legend and history, The Big Bad Wolf represents all the savage wolves of European legend, and the
Wicked Queen all the menacing women of power; this is the
first unveiling. But the threesome peels away another
layer: they transform themselves into three paunchy
businesspeople who literally smother Michael (Mickey) in a
surfeit of sweetness by stuffing his nose and mouth with
bonbons. Perhaps this is what Wolfe fears has happened to
all the powerful archetypes of fairy tales. They have been
transformed into sticky-sweet business ventures but, he
warns, such attempts to strip legends of their strength can
only provoke destruction. Hardly the lesson we customarily
receive from our childhood friend, Mickey Mouse, and his

57

colleagues.

"Alien Stones" (TIOD) practices a few turns of conventional expectations of those stock science-fiction characters, the capable and phlegmatic space ship captain and the eager young apprentice. When we see those characters we expect the former to teach us how the milieu of the story operates and the latter to keep us company in learning about it. We do not expect that the two may be the same person or that one of them exists only as a computer construct. Our expectations are upset further when the captain and his apprentice serve to make us question the story's reality rather than to present its reality to us. Such questions are especially surprising because the Captain does much that is quite expected: he falls in love with a beautiful passenger, induces the story's mystery by logical reasoning, and shows physical prowess and bravery.

Next to the observation that Gene Wolfe's work is underrated--an observation in the process of becoming obsolete--reviewers most often remark upon his use of children. The motif of the isolated child occurs again and again, early ("The Changeling," 1968, reprinted in GWBD), middle (Peace, 1975), and recent (The Shadow of the Torturer, 1980). An only child himself who has watched his own four children grow up, Wolfe has thought a great deal about childhood. The children he writes about are not the secure, fundamentally happy children often found in children's literature. His children remind us that childhood was far from carefree: the characters of Wolfe's stories are isolated, perhaps from family, perhaps from other children; they are outsiders to the adult world that towers over them; they are anxious, confused, and powerless to control a world bent upon disillusioning them. Though the children of Wolfe's fiction are not portrayed as typical or average, instead are insane, orphaned, damaged, brilliant, or wealthy, all readers who remember their childhoods remember their own feelings of isolation and anxiety as well as their frolicking and camaraderie. Wolfe concentrates upon those darker memories when he employs the motif of the isolated child.

How commonly does the isolated child occur in Wolfe's fiction? Here is a chronological list of his appearances: "Mountains Like Mice," "The Changeling," "Paul's Treehouse," "The Island of Doctor Death and Other Stories," Fifth Head of Cerberus, "Alien Stones," "The Death of Doctor Island," "Dark of the June," "The Hero as Werwolf," Peace, "Straw," The Devil in a Forest, "The Eyeflash Miracles," "Three Fingers," "The War Beneath the Tree," "The Adopted Father," and The Shadow of the Torturer. Almost always, the child is a boy--"The Dark of the June" is the only exception. His parents are dead ("The Changeling"), indifferent ("The Island of Doctor Death and Other Stories"), or absent ("The Eyeflash Miracles"); in some way his parents have failed as protectors. He is often an only child ("The Island of Doctor Death and Other Stories," Peace, "The War Beneath the Tree"), but sometimes merely separated from his siblings ("The Eyeflash Miracles"). He may be psychologically disturbed ("The Changeling," "The Death of Doctor Island"), or physically handicapped ("The Eyeflash Miracles"). Whatever his special difficulties, he is a child, and therefore powerless, unable to understand completely the adult world around him. As an orphan, an only child, a disturbed or broken one, he is isolated in some way from family, normality, and society. The isolation can signal and cause great distress, as it does in "The Changeling," or turn the isolato into a victim, as happens in "The Island of Doctor Death" trilogy, or bring about ecstasy and transformation, as occurs in "The Eyeflash Miracles."

In "The Changeling" (GWBD), a man convicted of treason during the Korean conflict returns to his home town and retreats into childhood memories. Memoir is an important device in Wolfe's work, used more elaborately in Fifth Head of Cerberus, Peace, and The Book of the New Sun. Peter Palmer, the story's narrator, comes home to a mystery and a dream. His hometown hasn't changed, children still play as they did when he was little, and as a childhood buddy says, "Nobody leaves Cassonville" (p. 142, GWBD). (The locale of Peace is Cassonville and the story previews the novel in various ways.) Peter Palmer discovers two strange things upon his return. First, there is no record of his having ever lived there: his father and mother are dead, his picture is missing in school photos, and whatever records of his life might have existed in the local newspaper have been burnt. Second, a little boy he remembers playing with as a child, a boy who was only four years old when Peter moved from Cassonville at about eight or nine, has now grown to be no more than eight or nine years old himself. That little boy's name is Peter Palmieri. Peter Palmer and Peter Palmieri exist simultaneously in the present of the story, and one other person, Peter Palmieri's adopted father, knows the boy has not aged according to the laws of real time. Within the limits of the story's reliability, then—and it is narrated by Palmer—strange things actually occur and remind us that this is a work of speculative fiction.

However, Palmer's life gives ample reason for his narration to be unreliable. His childhood was isolated: his mother died when he was eight or nine, and he and his father moved from Cassonville at that time, so he uses memory to escape into the time when he still had his mother, when he felt that he had a hometown. Peter Palmieri, his alter ego, never grows beyond the age at which Palmer lost his mother. Furthermore, Palmer's childhood was disturbing, as the following recollection shows:

> We had watched the little green animal hop back toward the water, and then, when it was only one jump away from dear safety, I had lashed out and suddenly, swiftly, driven the broad blade of my scout knife through him and pinned him to the mud. (p. 143, GWBD)

This impulsive, gratuitous, and irresponsible violence indicates an uneasy childhood, at the very least. Such a childhood, violent and lonely, might well have contributed to the adult's action of rejecting his native country to stay behind in Korea. The reverse of this logic is also true. Palmer's adult isolation, beginning with his father's death ("he was the last family I had, and things changed for me then," p. 140, GWBD), compounding in a Korean prison camp and later a U.S. military prison, might drive him back to a childhood which, however sad, would nevertheless be surrounded by the idyllic haze of recollection. In the Cassonville to which he returns, Palmer finds an eternal mother, Peter Palmieri's, whose child remains eternally a child. For Palmer, an escape into childhood would mean an escape into a time when he was not responsible for moral decisions. Peter Palmer and Peter Palmieri are the same person, Peter Pan refusing to grow up because of the threat of adult terrors and responsibilities.

In the "Island of Doctor Death" trilogy of novellas (TIOD)—which includes "The Island of Doctor Death and Other Stories," "The Death of Doctor Island," and "The Doctor of Death Island"—Wolfe shows a young child, an adolescent, and an adult, each isolated, each a victim, whose isolations are reflected by an island of some kind. Though the three protagonists are quite different people, living at different times and in different versions of the future, they also show how the isolated child grows up.

"The Island of Doctor Death and Other Stories" concerns a little boy who lives with his mother in a big house on an isthmus of land called Settlers Island. Tackman Babcock's mother is a drug addict who makes few allowances for "Tackie" in her life, so the lonely boy escapes into fiction, specifically into a lurid paperback called The Island of Doctor Death, which is a pulp transformation of H.G. Wells's The Island of Doctor Moreau with just a hint, in a hero named Ransom, of C.S. Lewis's <u>Out of the Silent Planet</u>. The novella combines excerpts from Tackie's reading with narration in the second person, "you" referring to Tackie as a representative child. Characters from the story Tackie is reading appear in the narration, as the child calls them up to keep him company. The strong and heroic Captain Ransom, the evil and powerful Doctor Death, and the faithful dog-man Bruno all become his companions. The first two have pale counterparts in Tackie's mundane life: Captain Ransom in the dashing but irresponsible Jason, the mother's boyfriend and supplier of drugs, and Doctor Death is Doctor Black, the mother's respectable and drab suitor, who saves her from a drug overdose but may also have supplied her with drugs. Unfortunately for Tackie, there is no counterpart in his exterior life for the faithful companion, except for his books—and his memories:

> Doctor Death smiles. "But if you start the book again we'll all be back. Even Golo and the bull-man."
> "Honest?"
> "Certainly." He stands up and tousles your hair. "It's the same with you, Tackie. You're too young to realize it yet, but it's the same with you." (p. 17, TIOD)

Tackie can relive his fantasies, in which vivid representations of good (Ransom) and evil (Death) take notice of him, and he can also recreate the events of his childhood later when he will have gained enough sophistication to understand the good, evil, and moral ambiguity of the adults who shaped his childhood through their indifference.

The adult Tackman Babcock will recall his lonely childhood from a safe distance, remembering not "as I watch, he pushes up my mother's sleeve" but the more remote "as you watch, he pushes up her sleeve so that all the other injection marks show" (p. 15, TIOD). He will know the difference between the realities and the fantasies of his childhood and be able to say:

> You run downstairs looking for Ransom, but he is gone and there is nobody at the party at all except the real people and, in the cold shadows of the back stoop, Doctor Death's assistant Golo. (p. 15, TIOD)

But he will also know that it was the fantasies that gave him the most companionship and the most intense vitality, not his mother who lived in her own dream world of drugs and in a place called "The House of 31 February." And we know that the narrator of this story is the adult Babcock recreating his puzzling childhood so that he can deal with it.

But if Tackie had possessed a psyche more frail or a family more damaging, what sort of adolescent might he have become? Perhaps he would have been as disturbed as Nicholas Kenneth de Vore, the protagonist of "The Death of Doctor Island." In this second in the trilogy of novellas, which received the 1973 Nebula Award, Nicholas is the fourteen-year-old son of a woman who lives in another sort of dream world:

> His mother had never been below the orbit of
> Mars, but she pretended to have spent her
> girlhood on Earth; each reference to the lie
> filled Nicholas with inexpressible fury and
> shame. (p. 108, TIOD)

Life and psyche have brought Nicholas to such a pass that he has spent a large portion of his short life in mental institutions. Because of his violence and visions, doctors have divided his brain in two, separating forever his left brain from his right. First isolated from his mother by her poor grasp of reality, then from her and the rest of society in mental institutions, and then from himself through brain surgery, Nicholas is now isolated along with a young girl, another seemingly hopeless mental invalid, on an artificial island. They are to serve as tools for the rehabilitation of a third person, Ignacio, who is seen as potentially a far more useful member of society. Nicholas has come to view the artificial island, Doctor Island, as his guide, protector, and healer, though it has insisted that it is merely a surrogate for society. When Nicholas realizes that Doctor Island is using him simply as a rehabilitative device for Ignacio and is willing to throw away Nicholas' life as it throws away the girl's to that end, Nicholas' rage shakes the island. The island retaliates by causing Nicholas to retreat completely into his right brain, becoming Kenneth the silent one, totally passive. The isolated child learns that society offers only two choices: usefulness or utter passivity. Since he cannot interact in a useful way with society, society makes his isolation complete.

"The Doctor of Death Island" offers more hope for the isolato. In this third variation on the motifs of isolates and islands, Wolfe shows an adult strong enough to have withstood the isolation of his childhood (his mother dead

62

before he was old enough to remember her, his father lost in religion and memories), the isolation of imprisonment, and the isolation of cryogenic freezing. Books saved Alvard as a child, because he surrounded himself with the characters of Dickens; books put him in prison, because he killed his business partner to keep control over his invention, speaking books; and books released him from prison, because his knowledgeable sabotage of the invention gave him bargaining power. Throughout his cryogenically extended life, Alvard retains his sanity and his ability to manipulate others. He is, then, someone who has not been broken by isolation, though he is not an exemplary figure either: he murdered his partner, and he booby-trapped his invention so that once a generation had become dependent upon it (speaking books make the actual ability to read them unnecessary), it would begin to deteriorate without his intervention. No Ben Franklin, he. Therefore, the novella's hope is not glorious: one may survive isolation but at a cost. Alvard lacks real empathy for anyone, including his lover. For him, people are no more real, perhaps less real, than the characters in his beloved Dickens.

In the first two novellas of this series, we could empathize with the lonely protagonists. In "The Doctor of Death Island," however, because of the protagonist's own lack of empathy, such engagement is not possible. Our inability to empathize with Alvard and his lack of vulnerability (surely these two features are connected) separate "The Doctor of Death Island" from the two earlier novellas, as does the introduction of the theme of immortality and the oddly jarring references to Dickens. The sum of these differences adds up to a less unified novella than either "The Island of Doctor Death and Other Stories" or "The Death of Doctor Island."

"The Eyeflash Miracles" (TIOD) uses many literary allusions, particularly to The Wizard of Oz, while its lonely boy, Little Tib, is empathetic to others and sympathetic to the reader with a vengeance. Though Wolfe does not allude to Dickens in this novella, the sentimental character of Little Tib, staunch, blind, and abandoned, is quite Dickensian indeed, and he shows a new, transcendentalist avatar of the isolated child. Here the child is betrayed by his parents and is an outcast of a harsh, dictatorial welfare system, left to wander alone and blind until two other outcasts of the system take him in. In spite of Little Tib's literal position as a victim, he is spiritually a victor, transcending his individual situation, and indeed mundane reality itself, by his divinity. He is Krishna and Christ the child, healing and walking on the air. Isolation, when it means one is an outlaw of an immoral government—as were Jesus fleeing into Egypt, Krishna hiding from King Kamsa, and Little Tib dodging the Office of Biogenetic Improvement—can purify rather than destroy or harden the individual. That is, it can if one is already an exceptional person, as these three are clearly meant to be.

In "The Eyeflash Miracles," Wolfe takes the isolated and damaged child, gives him special powers and a special destiny, and allows him finally to triumph, escaping those who would destroy him. Yet the novella ends with Little Tib rejoining Nitty, the Black man who befriended him at the story's beginning, walking along the railroad tracks, happy with their lot but still outcasts, both poor, one blind, on their way to Sugarland as if it were the promised land, or heaven. Little Tib may heal some people and inspire some others, but he remains an outcast from an unchanged, unregenerated world: happier, more cosmically significant, but no luckier in this world than Tackie Babcock. The isolated child may, in a rare and transcendental instance, offer salvation through his suffering, but he will not receive it himself.

The way to salvation, transcendental or otherwise, in Gene Wolfe's fiction, depends upon empathy: mutual understanding, compassion, and recognition of the other's humanity. But of what does humanity consist? That question becomes a recurring motif throughout Wolfe's work in "Trip Trap" (Orbit 2, ed. Knight), in "Eyebem" (Orbit 7, ed. Knight), in "The Toy Theater" (Orbit 9, ed. Knight, and TIOD), and in "The Fifth Head of Cerberus" (Orbit 10. ed. Knight, and FH), for example. One of Wolfe's most elaborate uses of the motif occurs in "Tracking Song" (TIOD). On the surface, "Tracking Song" is a rather gruesome and episodic tale: a man meets one humanoid species after another, eating some, on his quest for something called the "Great Sleigh." As usual in Wolfe's stories, however, there is more to deal with than the surface. First, it is a totem story:

> The protagonist gets his original orientation
> from a wolf tribe, then lives in a world in
> which the roles of moose, lion, deer, mink and
> so on are taken by semi-human beings. Wolves
> are winter symbols, of course, and birds symbols
> of spring.(4)

The people (we must call them that) with whom Cutthroat stays do not mimic every trait of their totems, but we do notice that the first group, the Wiggikki, sings and runs on

64

top of the snow, as wolves do. Nashwonk, with his size and his solitary habits, may be a bear. Perhaps the Pamigaka, who carry "short-handled tools with heavy, curved blades," and who eat many vegetables, are moose-totem people, or perhaps, because they are squat and build lodges, they are beaver-totem people (p. 188, TIOD). Mimmunka, who threatens them with "a polearm ending in cruel hooks" and has "huge green eyes that seemed too beautiful for a masculine face," seems certainly a lion-totem person (pp. 191-192, TIOD). Am Glowing, who runs, has dark eyes, is beautiful, and shares tribal affiliation with a man named Fishcatcher, takes the role of a mink. Later, Cutthroat meets vampires with human faces who are compared to birds. We cannot be positive of each person's affiliation, but it is true that when Cutthroat finally sees the Great Sleigh he asks: "who is that tall man with you? I think he has . . . wings?" (p. 236, TIOD). Whatever his affiliation, such a person possesses a distinctively bird-like attribute. This pattern of totems, Wolfe says, moves from winter to spring, just as the planet's weather gradually thaws in the course of the story.

There are other patterns as well. The narrator moves through a variety of cultures; from users of purely natural wood and stone tools, living in wooden lodges, closely attuned to the weather; to cave dwellers, whose bodies are partly mechanical and who live in decayed machine-age constructs awaiting the return of machine-age human beings; to those who have control over machinery and therefore over the weather itself, the inhabitants of the Great Sleigh who are, it is implied, responsible for "a reflector of bright, finely divided metal dust" which will bring spring to the wintery planet (p. 234, TIOD). People move from stone-age tools to primitive mechanisms or only partly understood use of machines to highly skilled use of science and technology.

Cutthroat also moves through a variety of belief systems, which might be taken as a lightning history of religion. In the first cultures he visits, religion serves to explain nature, and its rituals are meant to help the practitioners live in nature. In the cave of the half-mechanical people, religion serves to control people and is represented by a dictatorial leader. The people of the Great Sleigh may not have a religious system at all, but they do have an ethical system by whose logic they govern their behavior. One can see a parallel in movement between these three states of religious belief and those of Earth: first the pantheistic and shamanistic religions of the earliest people, then the stern monotheistic religions such as Judaism, Christianity, and Islam, and most recently such ethical systems as Deism and Existentialism.

These patterns bring us back to Wolfe's theme of the nature of humanity. The planet upon which Cutthroat travels is populated by humanoid species of varying levels of sentience, from vampires with human faces, to snow monkeys, to seemingly primitive peoples such as the Lenizee and the Pamigaka, to the more sophisticated Cutthroat, to the highly advanced inhabitants of the Great Sleigh. One might visualize this as a world in which all stages of human evolution coexist. None of the species here recognizes the humanity of any other species: "I am not an animal," says Cutthroat, and Longknife replies, "All the animals say that" (p. 179, TIOD). Yet each believes its own species to be human. We, sharing Cutthroat's opinion as he writes us his daily record, see most of the species as human, at least those with whom Cutthroat can speak. We find their dismissal of other speaking humanoids as inhuman not only unconvincing but savage: Wolfe describes one species eating another in a way which makes us think immediately of cannibalism—"I felt sick at the thought of eating the girl's flesh, no matter how inhuman she looked" (p. 177, TIOD). We know also that these speaking humanoids vary greatly in appearance from one another so that we then become uncertain about dismissing the humanity of those creatures with whom Cutthroat cannot speak, such as the snow monkeys. Where, we ask, does one draw the line between human and animal, sentient and unconscious? Where, in fact, does one draw the line between living and mechanical, for there are the Min to consider and the robots which (who?) help Cutthroat. Cutthroat recognizes the humanity in each person he meets, perhaps because, as an amnesiac, he does not know his own place in the order. Recognizing people's humanity, he chooses always to work cooperatively rather than competitively, whenever he has a choice.

That is the real message of Cutthroat's taped diary, which we (like the inhabitants of the Great Sleigh) are hearing. At present we do not confront other sentient species, nor do we yet deal with beings who make us question the division between living and mechanical. However, we constantly face other human beings who have alien religions, cultures, and levels of sophistication, and in our confrontations we consistently treat those human beings as if they were inhuman, subhuman. "Tracking Song" reminds us that calling another group of people inhuman, calling them gooks or niggers or honkies or slants, does not change the fact of their humanity. Instead, it turns life into an armed battle that empathy could transform into cooperation.

Each individual is, finally, an alien in the other's eyes. While empathy makes a bridge across the gulf between individuals, it cannot close the gap; perfect understanding is impossible. That becomes clear in Gene Wolfe's finest novella thus far, "Seven American Nights." Here a visitor to America struggles to understand its people, yet his own perceptual limitations keep him from even understanding what happens during his visit. We share Nadan Jaffarzadeh's struggle since the truth of events is embedded not only in the many layers of his perceptual limitations but in many layers of storytelling as well. Because this is a fiction, because despite the lucidity of the story's unfolding we cannot possibly determine an exact chain of events, we must ultimately realize that no final truth can be known. Perfect understanding of people, of events, of anything is impossible. This is not, however, a matter for despair;it is a recognition of the complexity of existence.

Wolfe expresses that complexity by building layers of perception as multifarious and as intriguing as any archaeologist could hope for. "Seven American Nights" is a frame tale reminding us that it has the power to alter what takes place within it. Only as we finish the novella do we realize how many frames Wolfe employs, for the story concludes with a dialogue between two women we assume to be Nadan's mother and his fiancee Yasmin. The dialogue is recorded by an outside voice, neither that of Nadan nor of the man who sent Nadan's diary to his mother. A chart will be the most succinct way to show the storytelling frames of this story.

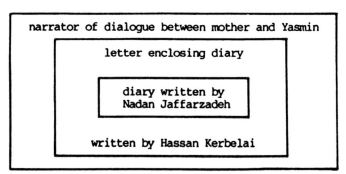

At each level we must learn new ways to question the reliability of the diary itself. In the dialogue, the older woman (Nadan's mother?) asks, "You think this is his writing?" and answers herself only "perhaps" (p. 410, TIOD). Perhaps the entire diary is a forgery. Next we examine the letter which encloses the diary. It is written by a private investigator who stands to gain monetarily only if there is reason to believe that Nadan still lives. The investigator, therefore, might forge all or part of the diary to encourage his client to continue the investigation. If the diary is entirely the work of Nadan Jaffarzadeh, it is still to be questioned. Nadan says that he has deleted those portions of the diary which reveal the purpose of his visit, though he does reveal a purpose at the end of his diary when he speculates that "I might seek to claim the miniatures of our heritage after all" (p. 409, TIOD). Furthermore, this lover of romance and drama reveals that he consciously alters his diary, when he says, "here I am not exaggerating or coloring the facts, though I confess I have occasionally done so elsewhere in this chronicle" (p. 401, TIOD).

Beyond these possible conscious alterations of the novella's central document, moreover, are those subconscious or unintentional alterations of events and motives which the diary's writer must inevitably impose. In any first person narrative, we know to question the narrator's reliability because we know that any witness is fallible. Here, however, our eyewitness is more fallible than usual. Nadan's perceptual accuracy must be questioned at many, many levels. First, he wears cultural blinders: he is a Moslem Iranian from a privileged culture visiting a decayed Western civilization whose attitudes toward religion, politics, and women, to name only three factors pertinent to the story, are quite different from his own. Next, we know that the same romantic and dramatic impulses that caused Nadan consciously to alter his diary might also direct him subconsciously. Further, Nadan tells us that he is on a secret mission and is suspicious of several of his shipboard companions because of it. His behavior can be explained either by an understandable suspicion of people who might be a genuine threat or by paranoia. If it is explained by paranoia, any or all of the remaining alterations of his perceptions may be caused only by his imagination. Many further alterations in Nadan's ability to perceive the world accurately are suggested in the unfolding of the story. Nadan suspects that he may have been given a mind-altering drug while aboard the ship to America and that tainted food may have caused hallucinations. On his first visit to the theater, he eats a candy egg with a peculiar taste: perhaps it, too, is tainted. Then, Nadan buys a hallucinogenic drug and impregnates one of the six remaining eggs, resolving to eat one each night, not knowing which contains the drug (which he suspects may actually be impotent), playing a sort of Russian roulette. We know that he eats five of the six eggs: his mind may be altered further on any one of these occasions, or on all, if all the eggs are tainted as the one

in the theater may have been. As for the sixth egg, Nadan
believes that the police have searched his room and stolen
it, but there is another explanation. The sixth egg may
have been the one containing the hallucinogen, and its effects may have caused him to lose a day. Our proof? "Seven
American Nights" describes only six nights.

Do the layers of perception stop here? Certainly not,
for Wolfe, or Nadan, introduces two scientific speculations
that would change Nadan's perception of reality. In the
first:

> Now we know that there is only one particle of
> each variety [neutron, positron, and electron],
> moving backward and forward in time, an electron
> when it travels as we do, a positron when its
> temporal displacement is retrograde, the same
> few particles appearing billions of billions of
> times to make up a single object, and the same
> few particles forming all the objects, as it
> were, of the same set of pastels. (p. 366,
> TIOD)

Matter is, then, impermanent and insubstantial, existing
only in the present moment, as if neo-Platonic angels were
hectically rebuilding the universe before our eyes. Such a
theory, incidentally, justifies the use of diary format, for
it concerns itself with each day as it occurs rather than in
insubstantial retrospect.

While Nadan claims universal acceptance ("now we know
. . . ") for the first theory, the second one is entirely
his own.

> Tonight, when we walked beneath its [the old
> highway's] ruined overpasses, they seemed inex-
> pressibly ancient and sinister. It occurred to
> me then that there may be a time-flaw, such as
> astronomers report from space, somewhere in the
> Atlantic. How is it that this western shore is
> more antiquated in the remains of a civilization
> not yet a century dead than we are in the shadow
> of Darius? May it not be that every ship that
> plows the sea moves through ten thousand years?
> (p. 372, TIOD)

Perhaps such a speculation belongs more to romance than to
science, yet the reader cannot help but notice that
Washington's decay seems more extensive than 100 years could
explain. The two speculations, if taken as scientific,

69

remind us that Wolfe's work is categorized as science fiction; if taken as romantic, that it defies categorization. Scientific or romantic, the two speculations further complicate any determination of a specific, independently observable chain of events.

Wolfe does not build so many layers of perception and of storytelling to fool us, though there is about his stories an aura of the intellectual puzzle. Such complexity mimics the human condition: all our lives are spent trying to determine the truth of events and motives, to pierce through barriers raised by our minds and cultures. We never succeed, but we may learn a good deal in the course of the struggle. "Seven American Nights" makes us struggle, but it teaches us as well. Any lesson about the human condition sounds platitudinous and shallow in its simple statement. The struggle to attain the lesson, or the struggle during which it is absorbed, gives it its profundity. "Seven American Nights" is an Easter story that avoids platitude and sentiment, both common pitfalls of rebirth stories.

The last day which Nadan describes is Easter Day, and all the events of the novella have led up to it. On each day of his visit, he eats a candy egg, one of the symbols of Easter and rebirth. On Easter Day, he comes upon an Easter procession that takes on symbolic meaning for him.

> When the old priest [who leads the procession] was born, the greatness of America must have been a thing of such recent memory that few can have realized it had passed forever; and the entire procession—from the flickering candles in clear sunshine, to the dead leader lifted up, to his inattentive, bickering followers behind— seemed to me to incarnate the philosophy and the dilemma of these people. So I felt, at least, until I saw that they watched it as uncomprehendingly as they might if they themselves were only travelers abroad, and I realized that its ritualized plea for life renewed was more foreign to them than to me. (p. 408, TIOD)

Throughout his visit, Nadan has searched for an apt symbol of America; the eagle is now extinct, and Nadan puts in its place first the nightmare and then its incarnation, the actress Ardis. As he watches the procession, he sees in it a representation of America's essence, its determined individualism combined with its equal determination to act collectively. He believes that the participants have no hope or even understanding of a reborn nation. For Nadan,

70

Easter has no message for America. His own country, Iran, is at the apex of power and wealth: from that height, it is impossible for him to see any signs of birth at the nadir.

Those readers who are members of America before the fall look hard for a signs of rebirth in the rubble that Wolfe describes, and they can be found. At the Washington theater, drama is being revived: art arises from the decay. The American natives put much hope in the possibilities of a secret hidden beneath Mount Rushmore; Nadan speculates that the secret may be the knowledge of the ability to grasp a trend, grapple with it, and control it. Whatever the secret, perhaps the stone will roll back and the saving secret will be revealed: the Easter setting offers hope. When Nadan first meets Ardis, he associates her with eggs, which are, of course, symbols of birth and Easter. Later he rejects her, and kills her, because he finds that she possesses a deformity. She is mortal, vulnerable, and imperfect like the others. But perhaps Nadan's first impression was correct, and Ardis, in her imperfection, nevertheless does represent an America rising out of its ashes. She is dead, but there are many like her, and perhaps some kind of revitalization is evolving from these mutated people. Perhaps. This story does not have the triumphant strain of optimism so often found in Christian stories of rebirth. The emphasis upon decay and struggle makes clear that renaissance is slow, difficult, and hard-earned.

"Seven American Nights" addresses Americans as they live their lives now, because it shows wherein rebirth lies--in creative effort and in determination--how modestly it begins and with what struggle it unfolds itself. This vision of the commonly-employed theme shuns the usual pathos of death and the fanfare of transfiguration, which we have come to expect in stories of rebirth, a pattern which lurks in "The Eyeflash Miracles." Instead, Wolfe uses one of the conventions of science fiction, life-after-the-apocalypse, and inverts a couple of other literary conventions; 1001 Arabian Nights, another frame tale, is transferred West and becomes "Seven American Nights," and the Western traveler to the exotic decayed East, whom we remember from Sir Richard Burton, T.E. Lawrence, and even Richard Haliburton, is transformed into an Eastern traveler visiting a strange and crumbling Occident. Wolfe turns all these conventional themes and forms them into a story distinctively his own. That transformation is one reason for the judgment that it is his finest short work. There are other reasons as well.

"Seven American Nights" satisfies first at the level of plot. It contains adventure and romance, horrible monsters, beautiful ladies, and a convincing view of a crum-

71

bling Washington, rooted in the city's present geography and decaying in believable ways. The plot leads us to a complex statement about life, as we have already seen. The diary form, with its expressions of the narrator's perceptual quirks and limitations, gives a clear vision of Nadan Jaffarzadeh's character: a bit vain, suspicious, intelligent, adventure-seeking, romantic, yet cautious and conservative withal. More remarkable is Wolfe's control over the many layers of perception and narration of the story, resulting in a purposeful ambiguity that nevertheless retains sharp clarity. Wolfe sometimes allows his ambiguity to turn into obscurity ("To the Dark Tower Came")(5) or a simple mental puzzle ("Cherry Jubilee")(6). At his best, as in "Seven American Nights," from puzzle and mystery arises beauty, not frustration. In the best of Gene Wolfe's short works, as here—and I would add to that list such uncollected stories as the four Continuum stories, "The Detective of Dreams" in Kirby McCauley's Dark Forces anthology, and "The Last Thrilling Wonder Story" in the June 1982 Isaac Asimov's Science Fiction Magazine—Gene Wolfe demonstrates that science fiction can hold its own according to the most exacting standards of science fiction and academe.

NOTES

(1)   "The Woman Who Loved the Centaur Pholus," Isaac Asimov's Science Fiction Magazine, December 1979, pp. 108-118.
(2)   "House of Ancestors," IF, June 1968, pp. 101-120.
(3)   "The HORARS of War," Nova 1, ed. Harry Harrison (New York: Delacorte, 1970).
(4)   Joan Gordon, "An Interview With Gene Wolfe," Science Fiction Review, Summer 1981, p. 19.
(5)   "To the Dark Tower Came," in Orbit 19, ed. Damon Knight (New York: Harper, 1977), pp. 120-125.
(6)   "Cherry Jubilee," Isaac Asimov's Science Fiction Magazine, 18 Jan. 1982, pp. 108-135.

VIII

THE BOOK OF THE NEW SUN

With the publication of The Shadow of the Torturer,
the first volume of The Book of the New Sun, Gene Wolfe's
reputation changed from that of a good but obscure science-
fiction writer to that of a good and famous one. All four
volumes have made the Locus science-fiction best seller
list, as have the short story collections published after
The Shadow of the Torturer. Though Wolfe may have been
facetious when he claimed that he wrote the tetralogy partly
so science-fiction fans would masquerade in costumes inspired by it, he probably did want the popularity such
masquerade implies. Whether or not anyone has yet gone to a
convention in Severian's fuligen cape, The Book of the New
Sun has brought a much wider popularity than was Wolfe's
before. Every volume has been nominated for the Hugo and
Nebula awards. The Shadow of the Torturer won the 1981
World Fantasy Award and the British Science Fiction Society
Award, The Claw of the Conciliator won the 1981 Nebula
Award, and The Sword of the Lictor won Locus' 1983 Best Fantasy Novel Award. Wolfe has served as guest of honor at
many science-fiction conventions, and his name appears
prominently on any magazine cover that encloses one of his
stories. Should blurbs with his name begin to appear on new
books by other science-fiction authors, his status in
science fiction will be firmly entrenched.
    The Book of the New Sun consists of The Shadow of the
Torturer, The Claw of the Conciliator, The Sword of the Lictor, and The Citadel of the Autarch. Wolfe is writing a
fifth companion volume, a coda to the tetralogy called The
Urth of the New Sun, and has already written a book about
writing The Book called The Castle of the Otter (he is planning a second volume called Return to the Castle of the
Otter). Every published volume, including the limited edi-
tion Castle, has met with strong reviews and lively sales:
all hardback first editions quickly sold out, and all
volumes have been reprinted by the Science-Fiction Book
Club. Among the most thoughtful reviews of the tetralogy
are Colin Greenland's review of the first two volumes in
Foundation, Elizabeth Hull's overview in Extrapolation, Algis Budrys' series of reviews on each volume in The Magazine
of Fantasy and Science Fiction, and John Clute's front-page
review of The Citadel of the Autarch, combined with Michael
Dirda's interview with Wolfe, in the Washington Post Book

73

World.(1)

Gerald Jonas of the New York Times Book Review waited until the release of The Citadel of the Autarch to review the series but gave it unqualified praise when the review came, saying of Wolfe:

> the publication of his brilliant "The Fifth Head of Cerberus" in 1972 earned him a place among a small band of accomplished stylists in science fiction, along with Samuel R. Delany, Thomas M. Disch, Joanna Russ and one or two others. The completed "Book of the New Sun" establishes his pre-eminence, pure and simple.(2)

Baird Searles, in Isaac Asimov's Science Fiction Magazine, agrees with Jonas and adds that The Book of the New Sun "will undoubtedly be considered a landmark in the field," but he goes on to wonder whether, "under that glittering edifice of surprising words and more surprising events and characters . . . [there is] a story or a concept of any stature."(3) It seems clear to me that there is a story though not an uncommon one, and a number of concepts, including some very important ones. Searles' question reflects a certain consternation with Wolfe's baroque and indirect approach to a genre more commonly represented by a plain style and direct approach.

The plot (the story) of The Book of the New Sun is straightforward and at first glance, unexceptional. A young man is exiled from his guild but given a powerful sword and a book that contains the secrets of life. He finds a miraculous gem and goes on a quest to return it to its rightful owners. He has many adventures along the way and at the end of them is made king and is about to save the world: a coming-of-age story, a quest story, an adventure story, a success story, and a save-the-world story. There are, then, plenty of story-elements in The Book, though none of them is unusual. But rarity does not give stories their stature—most of the great literature of the world runs on such ordinary plots as love, revenge, coming of age, and questing. Are the stories written with graceful and powerful control, placed within a fully-realized world, acted out by satisfying characters, made significant by their illustration of fascinating and important ideas or concepts? If so, the work as a whole has stature; The Book of the New Sun has such stature. This chapter will support the claim of the tetralogy's value by examining its style, setting, characterization, and themes. Each of these categories is separate from the others only through academic convention, of course, and each will be discussed separately with the constant acknowledgment that it exists to enhance the other elements of the book and to help form a complex and unified work.

Style, for example, articulates Wolfe's vision of Earth and Urth. The term "baroque," which has frequently been applied to his work, applies not only to language and sentence structure of The Book, to its giantism in imagery and to its maze structure, but to the elaborate and convoluted society Wolfe describes, the abundance of characters, most of whom undergo many variations on their basic stereotypes and archetypes as they develop, and the rich counterpoint of themes, both speculative and philosophical. "Baroque" even suggests religion's role in the novel.

"Baroque" often refers to the elaborate and the convoluted; opposite to the plain, unadorned style of Hemingway, often employed in science fiction, baroque style in science fiction includes unusual, esoteric language and complicated, indirect--indeed, almost tortured--sentence structure. The tetralogy's first chapter introduces us to Wolfe's baroque language and sentence structure. Barbican, gallipots, mystes, badelaire, oblesque, dholes, amschaspand: every word is strange to the twentieth-century ear, many are unknown to the common reader, yet all are in the lexicon. In his appendix to the first volume, Wolfe says:

> in rendering this book--originally composed in a tongue that has not yet achieved existence--into English, I might easily have saved myself a great deal of labor by having recourse to invented terms; in no case have I done so. Thus in many instances I have been forced to replace yet undiscovered concepts by their closest twentieth-century equivalents. Such words as pelast, androgyn, and exultant, are substitutions of this kind, and are intended to be suggestive rather than definitive. (Appendix, p. 302, ST)

This paragraph indicates several reasons why Wolfe chose to use esoteric language though it might alienate certain readers, or, as he puts it in The Castle of the Otter,

> some fans seem to be able to tolerate any amount of gibberish, so long as it is gibberish; but let a hard-working writer venture some perfectly legitimate word like epopt, and-- . . . . . ("Words Weird and Wonderful," p. 26, CO)

First of all, the use of esoteric words rather than made-up ones forges a link between the tetralogy's Urth and our world, while at the same time conveying "the flavor of an odd place at an odd time" ("Words Weird and Wonderful", p. 26, CO). The words are peculiar, yes, but they belong to our culture. Second, the use of words from the past to indicate future concepts reminds us not only that Severian's Urth in some ways resembles our Earth of the distant past with its terminology and conventions based on Roman legions and medieval castles, but that time in these books is not strictly linear. Past words convey future concepts in a world where the author can translate works "surviving so many centuries of futurity" (Appendix, p. 303, ST), where the novels' characters can search for one another up and down corridors of time, where the protagonist can also exist as his own ancestor. Third, invented terms would refer exclusively and specifically to Wolfe's invented concepts whereas his speculation and vision are meant to be "suggestive rather than definitive." Fourth, Wolfe's real words suggest a broad knowledge—of military history, weaponry, architecture, pharmacy, alchemy, zoology, comparative religion, and of course, torture—which gives the tetralogy a feeling of depth, solidity, vastness, and complexity far beyond its sheer bulk of pages. Such a feeling, of much going on at once, and in an aesthetically and logically satisfying way, is at the heart of the baroque.

Sentence structure functions in The Book of the New Sun much as its language does, not to obfuscate but to illustrate. Again, let the tetralogy's first chapter exemplify:

> It is possible I already had some presentiment of my future. The locked and rusted gate that stood before us, with wisps of river fog threading its spikes like the mountain paths, remains in my mind now as the symbol of my exile. That is why I have begun this account of it with the aftermath of our swim, in which I, the torturer's apprentice Severian, had so nearly drowned. (Ch. 1, p. 9, ST)

Though the first sentence is fairly short (eleven words), it nevertheless proceeds from present tense (is) to past (had) and ends with the word "future," showing us that time will not be linear in the tetralogy. The two remaining sentences are much longer (thirty-two words and twenty-seven words). In the first of these two longer sentences, the subject

76

(gate) is separated from the verb (remains) by a long (sixteen word) string of qualifications. Which gate? the one "that stood before us"; how did it stand? "with wisps of river fog"; what was that fog doing? "threading its spikes"; and what was that action like? "mountain paths." The sentence has moved from a gate to a mountain path, duplicating Severian's later travels, before returning to its anchoring verb, as Severian eventually returns to Nessus: Severian's journey to the throne will be no more straightforward. In this sentence the fog is altered by a simile, the gate becomes a symbol; nothing is permitted to remain definitive, all becomes suggestive. The last sentence of the paragraph, which explains the why of what has gone before, leaves us nevertheless <u>in media res</u>, asking, what swim? what torturer? what drowning? Time is again disjointed: "have begun," "aftermath," "had drowned." And the crucial, most active verb of the sentence, though not the independent one, "had drowned," is saved for the end of the sentence. Working through the sentence is like following a mountain path or maze. The sentence, typical of the baroque sentence structure of the novels, though grammatically in perfect control, operates not only to present information but to duplicate the protagonist's journey, which is made complex not only by the convolutions of its outward events but by the branchings of the traveler's prodigious memories.

Severian's memory is indeed prodigious: he claims to forget nothing. Much of this Urth is prodigious. The Citadel in which Severian has lived his whole life looms so large that he keeps coming upon corridors he has never seen before. Somewhere in that Citadel, and extending a vast distance beyond, is a huge library. Outside the Citadel lies the gigantic city of Nessus and through it flows the vast river Gyoll. Somewhere outside the gates of Nessus, the armies of the Commonwealth and of its enemy, the Ascians, flow endlessly into battle in hundreds of thousands. Severian meets the giant Baldanders and the two-headed giant Typhon. He scales gigantic mountains carved with monstrous figures. It is all very well to say that the land Wolfe describes must be South America, since several clues tell us it is south of the equator, that it has a broad pampas (rather than a plain or outback or veldt), that its natives have skin that is dark but not black, and so on. But these clues, though they connect Earth to Urth, also remind us, as the esoteric language does, that the world of the novels is "an odd place at an odd time." Wolfe's repeated use of giantism in his imagery lends oddness to his Urth. And like his use of peculiar vocabulary, these images function in other ways as well. They fit the scale of the tetralogy.

Four volumes, 1222 pages in the first editions, all to produce what Severian surprises us by describing as "this too-brief account of a summer more than normally turbulent" (Ch. 37, p. 308, CA). The prodigiousness of the images matches the scale of Severian's memory. The vastness of the artifacts of Severian's time also reflects the vast distance of "so many centuries of futurity."

If, in the baroque era, Versailles' scale reminded people of the huge gulf separating the rulers from those they ruled, then in Severian's era, the huge scale of the House Absolute can serve as a similar reminder: size and political power are connected in many of the tetralogy's images of giantism. If, in the baroque era, the vastness of St. Peter's Basilica reminded people of their position in the cosmos, the sheer giantism of such natural phenomena as the River Gyoll and the broad pampas serve a similar function in Severian's time. Size serves in Severian's age as it did in the baroque--to emphasize the gulf between ordinary human beings and the seats of power, both political and spiritual. The giantism of such artificial constructs as Typhon's carved mountain attempts to prove humanity's ability to control nature, a desire sympathetic with the control over natural forces sought in that far earlier baroque time.

But there is another kind of vastness, that of multiplicity, which operates in The Book's imagery and to which the term "baroque" applies. The hordes of armies, the numbers of cacogens, the kinds of genetically engineered animals, the variety of cultures, and of customs and guilds within Severian's culture, all woven together into these four volumes, form a complex unity like the contrapuntal forms of baroque music or like the topiary mazes of which baroque palace-builders were fond.

Images of giantism are not the only repeated images of the novels: gates, caves, roses, claws, cannibalism, suns, light and shadow, the colors black, white, and red appear again and again. They are all symbols of life, death, and rebirth, often with Christian associations, reminding us of the novels' thematic concerns at the same time their recurrence leads us down pattern-forming paths, as if we followed a maze. The baroque multiplicity of paths leads us in various ways to the center, the core of the novels' meaning, though we cannot always see where we are headed or to what. Other symbols and images recur in the tetralogy. Characters appear, disappear, reappear again: Agia, Triskele, Master Malrubius, Rudesind, the Green Man, Dr. Talos. They carry with them, in their comings and goings, threads of plot, so that eventually all are woven into a complex tapestry. They bring with them reminders of their earlier appearances in Severian's life, so that we are conscious of how Severian himself has changed. We have a true sense of their running through corridors of time, as some of them are described as doing, because they dodge in and out of our memories in a similar fashion as we read.

The effect of all these recurrences of people, symbols, and images is similar to the effects of similar repetitions in the Labyrinths of Borges. The Book of the New Sun builds labyrinths of words, images, and ideas just as its protagonist follows a labyrinthine path to the Pelerines, to the autarchy, to the New Sun. As we follow the mazes, we look for more clues, more recurrences, searching for the patterns which will lead us to meaning. And each time we find another appearance of Agia, another rose, another giant, we feel echoes from our past with the novel, as Severian the memorious (who shares his talent for remembering with Borges' "Funes the Memorious") feels echoes, reminders, reverberations from his past at each stage of his journey. Severian describes his personality, once it contains not only his memories and Thecla's, but those of the Autarch "who in one body is a thousand" (Ch. 27, p. 224, CA), in this way.

> The old, simple structure of my single personality was no more; but the new, complex structure no longer dazzled and bewildered me. It was a maze, but I was the owner and even the builder of that maze. (Ch. 30, pp. 242-243, CA)

Severian's memoriousness forms a maze; so does the multiplicity of his memories. The fictive writing of this four-volume memoir puts him in possession of the labyrinths of his memory, and Severian feels similar control over the maze of his personality.

Another kind of Borgesian maze recurs in The Book: the embedded story. Such stories include not just Severian's dreams and Thecla's embedded memories, and the appendices that accompany each volume, but seven self-contained stories. The tetralogy's second volume (Volume One contains no stories of this kind) holds two tales: "The Tale of the Student and His Son" (Ch. 17), which Severian reads from Thecla's brown book to comfort his injured friend Jonas; and "Dr. Talos's Play: Eschatology and Genesis" (Ch. 24), which the company performs at the House Absolute. Volume Three contains just one intercalated story, "The Tale of the Boy Called Frog" (Ch. 19), again from the brown book, this time read by Severian to comfort little Severian.

79

Volume Four contains the most stories, four tales told in a contest to win Foila's hand. The stories are "Hallvard's Story—The Two Sealers" (Ch. 7), "Melito's Story—The Cock, the Angel, and the Eagle (Ch. 9), "Loyal to the Group of Seventeen's Story—The Just man" (Ch. 11), and, an unexpected twist, "Foila's Story—The Armiger's Daughter" (Ch. 13).

Because I have discussed at length Wolfe's use of the embedded story elsewhere (see the chapters on The Fifth Head of Cerberus and Peace), here I wish only to mention how these embedded stories form another kind of figurative maze in the tetralogy. When we fall into one of these stories, it seems to be leading us away from the main path, but when we clamber out at the end of the story, we find that it has actually led us further on by a circuitous route. In revealing the character of the teller and his or her culture, in its reiteration of the tetralogy's major symbols (such as the maze in "The Tale of the Student and His Son") and themes (such as the value of simplicity and honesty in Foila's story), each story moves us deeper toward the center of the maze. It does so in a non-linear way, replicating the non-linear vision of time by which The Book operates.

Figurative mazes are echoed by architectural ones in The Book: the Citadel, the library, the botanical garden, the House Absolute, the dungeons beneath it, the cave of the man-apes, the walled city of Thrax, and so on and on. This is but one way that setting confirms style and directs us to theme in the tetralogy. If the style of these novels may be equated with the baroque, so may the setting. Wolfe says,

> for years before I began reading sf . . ., I had been following Flash Gordon's adventures on the immense planet Mongo; and as a result I was often irritated (as I still am) when I discovered a writer assuming a single, simple, uniform culture covering an entire world. . . . I find this both incredible and boring (a poor but only too possible combination). I wanted to show an entire society: one I could attempt to make plausibly complex. ("Helioscope," pp. 8-9, CO)

His orchestration of the various cultures and subcultures that make up the Commonwealth and Ascians of Urth is a contrapuntal, a baroque exercise. We learn that the Commonweath has a caste system, each caste with its own culture, and that it has a number of guilds, each with its own societal structure. We find that the people of the pampas, of the cities of Nessus and Thrax and the village of Saltus, of

80

the jungle, of the mountain paths, of the floating islands, each have their own culture within the Commonwealth. The innumerable Ascians have their own cultures as well, brilliantly suggested by "Loyal to the Group of Seventeen's Story—The Just Man" (Ch. 11, CA). All these cultures, so different from one another, nevertheless form together the baroque future Wolfe has imagined.

This future Urth, though it shares geographic basics with our Earth, also possesses a wealth of diverse new features: huge mountains layered with human, not geologic history; vast caverns formed by ancient cities and subway systems; the marvelous floating islands; the complex currents of the rivers. The people of Urth form various races based on caste or geography. The animals around them are quite changed from those of Earth, due to genetic engineering and extra-terrestrial imports, but they are many. Wolfe's baroque vision of Urth is not only immense, but diverse as well.

And not only diverse, but complex: Wolfe's handling of characterization is especially contrapuntal and maze-like, dynamic and compelling. The characters begin as stereotypes and archetypes, but these types develop gradually and surprisingly into transformed versions of those types. These evolving types change, seem to change, reveal unchanged selves in changing ways, so that our evaluations of them keep changing as well. We follow clues as the characters appear and reappear throughout the volumes: now he is good, now evil; now she is right, now wrong.

Vodalus is a character who reveals his unchanged self in changing ways. His first appearance, drawing his sword in the graveyard at night to protect a beautiful woman, is glamorous and mysterious. Seen through Severian's eyes, he is heroic: the type of the noble outlaw, fighting against oppression. In Volume Two, Severian has the opportunity to see the ruthlessness of Vodalus' methods and to evaluate the quality of his followers: outlaw, yes—but noble, not particularly. By Volume Three, Severian has forsaken his guild and the past it represents; he must, then, reject the past Vodalus wants to recall. And by Volume Four, we see Vodalus as noble again, at least in comparison to Agia, though wrong. Agia, by the way, is the most static character in the book, though she dons many masks. Ruled by revenge, she retains a consistent measure of hatred for Severian throughout the tetralogy.

Baldanders seems to change, from the gentle, slavish giant of Volume One to the violent but confused one of Volume Two to the brilliant and dangerous one of Volume

Three. His behavior is markedly different in each volume, yet we finally realize that each version of Baldanders is present in the others and we are watching the slow process of the giant's coming awake, becoming aware, coming of age, seen at intervals. Our view of Baldanders shifts from giant as gentle beast to cruel ogre, from one type to another, though the giant himself combines both types.

The most complex handling of character in The Book of the New Sun, however, involves Severian's development from torturer to potential savior and his changing views of women. His handling of Severian's character, and through Severian, of several female characters, shows how important Wolfe's baroque techniques of characterization are for illuminating the world of the story and the vision behind the world.

Severian doesn't seem to change; he really does change. How? Most obviously, he ages from an innocent adolescent to a world-worn man, though this aging occurs in the space of less than a year. The unquestioning torturer's apprentice of the first volume, who offers death to the woman he loves and sees other women as temptresses or as helpless children, was raised in an exclusively male enclave. His knowledge of women, and of relationships between the sexes, is based almost entirely upon hearsay and forced situations until he is exiled from the guild. When, in Chapter 26, "Sennet," of The Shadow of the Torturer, he analyzes the difference between desire and love for women, he speaks from very little experience. Later analyses in later volumes are more convincing.

Severian is sexist--because his world is sexist--but he and his world are changing. Severian's Urth--decaying, decadent, losing energy, living on its past--must change. Severian, though courageous, witty, and honorable, is a product of that world and will be as decadent and backward as his society until he sees the light.

Though Severian is an attractive person with sharp perceptions and an infallible memory, his specific upbringing as well as his society make him an unreliable narrator; his moral center is skewed. Wolfe performs an impressive feat in causing us to sympathize with a torturer, to find reasonable his arguments for the validity of torture as a tool of justice. But we are not meant to stay convinced. In Chapter 29, "Agilus," of the first volume, Severian strikes Agia and pushes her against a stone wall. His behavior is violent and his reaction to Agia's pain quite without passion. Such violence and cold-bloodedness are meant to be repellent. We are supposed to come to our senses and see beneath the attraction; torture is a wicked means that invalidates the justice it is meant to serve, and cold-blooded violence signifies clearly a moral flaw. Severian gradually comes to realize this, becoming more compassionate as the tetralogy unfolds, and vowing in the last volume, as Autarch, to eliminate the torturers' guild.

Likewise, as Severian learns more and more about women, he sees them less as types and more as human beings. Thecla, once she becomes a part of Severian after the ceremony of the alzabo, changes him from an isolate male to an androgynous character who contains both male and female qualities as well as memories. Once this transformation begins, ignorant stereotyping becomes increasingly untenable, until, by the end of the last volume, Severian's mind contains not only his own memories and Thecla's, which have become stronger in each volume, but those of countless other men and women who have been Autarch.

Still, the Severian of Volume One is a sadistic sexist, though appealing enough despite it that a woman wrote Wolfe describing Severian as "rather a sweet boy." Partly because of the many adventures and ordeals of the circular journey from Nessus to Nessus that teach him and mature him and partly because his memory allows him to reflect on what he has learned, Severian changes from the rather sweet sadist of Volume One to the compassionate man of Volume Four who is wise and open enough to receive the significance of the Claw. But another significant reason that Severian is transformed is because of his relationships with women. Three of these relationships are particularly telling: the ones with Thecla, Jolenta, and Dorcas.

When Severian first meets Thecla, she is a client of the torturers, a prisoner. The naive, romantic, and isolated Severian sees her as a tall, beautiful, aloof moon-goddess figure whom he comes to love "for her condescension in submitting to us" (Ch. 26, p. 232, ST). He does not understand her or even humanize her, but his idealized love compels him to allow her the release of suicide. In giving Thecla a knife, Severian sees himself as betraying his guild, not as performing a compassionate act. In Volume Two, Severian consumes Thecla's flesh and incorporates her memories with his own:

> She was there, filling me as a melody fills a cottage. . . . I learned what it was for one who had never seen a cell or felt a whip to be prisoner of the torturers, what dying meant, and death. . . . We were one, naked and happy and clean, . . . with woven hair [we] read from a single book. (Ch. 11, pp. 99-100, CC)

Having done this, having experienced the life of a woman and a client, Severian's view of women and of his career is altered. He is still capable of sexism and cruelty--the change is not sudden or complete--but it does begin: he is no longer devoted to Vodalus' quest for the past, he experiences slight guilt after killing a man ("I could not escape the eerie feeling that he was in some sense watching me, the man who had killed him to save himself," Ch. 13, p. 109, CC), he begins to recognize the evil of his profession. And he begins to understand more compassionately the kinship of love and desire in his relationships with women, understanding at the same time that his view of the feminine ideal is not the real woman. Thecla, who makes Severian both male and female, catalyzes his enlightenment, makes him receptive to it when events and people present him with enlightening information.

Jolenta, who single-mindedly yet mindlessly oozes sex, seems an unlikely candidate to raise Severian's consciousness, but his examination of his reactions to her in Volume Two teaches him much about the difference between women as objects and women as autonomous individuals. Although Jolenta began as an ordinary, rather plain waitress in Volume One, Dr. Talos has transformed her into an incredibly voluptuous, sexual, and sensual caricature of woman as sex-object. She is now an artificial construct, the real woman completely buried by the perfumed flesh. A man (an artificial construct himself) has made her literally into what men have often attempted to make women. She is a kind of monster of desire, and, when she and Severian couple in the garden of the House of Absolute, Severian's reaction is monstrous:

> Jolenta's desire was no more than the desire to
> be desired, so that I wished, not to comfort her
> loneliness . . , nor to find expression for an
> aching love. . . , not to protect her . . . ,
> but to shame and punish her, to destroy her
> self-possession, to fill her eyes with tears and
> tear her hair as one burns the hair of corpses
> to torment the ghosts who have fled them. (Ch.
> 13, p. 207, CC)

He recognizes, then, that a being which exists only as a sex object is no more real or lovable than a corpse from which the soul has fled.

But without Dr. Talos to refurbish her, Jolenta deteriorates, the opulent flesh "softened like wax" until,

84

dying, "she seemed a flower too long blown" (Ch. 28, pp. 267-268, CC). Only then,

> when desire had fled and I could only look at
> Jolenta with pity, I found that though I had
> believed I cared only for her importunate, rose-
> flushed flesh and the awkward grace of her move-
> ments, I loved her. (Ch. 28, p. 269, CC)

He can love the human being, not the object, and, more importantly, he understands the difference.

While Severian knows Jolenta for only a short time, however, Dorcas appears in every volume of Severian's journey. Dorcas becomes the most fully human to him of all the female characters and therefore the most deeply loved of all the women he meets. Dorcas is the recipient of Severian's first miracle with the Claw: until she touched Severian's hand in the lake of the Garden of Endless Sleep, she had been lying dead beneath the lake's embalming water. She saves Severian from drowning, he brings her back to life; they begin on equal footing despite Severian's still-immature, initial perception of Dorcas as a frail and confused child-woman. Though he and Dorcas are soon separated at the gate of Nessus, he realizes that she is already "more than a lover, a true companion" (Ch. 35, p. 295, ST). He is capable of this realization even before Thecla's memory opens him to androgyny, but afterward he is further opened not only to Dorcas's companionship but to her protection: I want to protect you from the opinion of the world," she says (Ch. 22, p. 199, CC). She helps him understand that he can change, that he need not symbolize death in his torturer's habit:

> To me you're Life, and you're a young man named
> Severian, and if you wanted to . . . become a
> carpenter or a fisherman, no one could stop you.
> (Ch. 22, p. 200, CC)

No one else but Dorcas understands his potential for change, for enlightenment. Only she can allow the possible progression of meanings for Severian's name—from severe to sever to savior. Only she who "had been my counselor in perplexity and my comrade in a hundred desert places" can provide "moral shelter" for Severian (Ch. 1, p. 14, SL). Dorcas helps him understand the relationship between Dr. Talos and Baldanders, the nature of the Claw's action, and the meaning of true friendship in which each person helps and accepts help from the other.

It seems especially hard that they must separate, as
they do a third of the way through Volume Three.   Dorcas,
having recalled something of her life before the Garden of
Endless Sleep, must return to that life to complete her
past, while Severian must continue on his quest to return
the Claw to the Pelerines to fulfill his destiny.   Her coun-
sel has helped the memorious and androgynous Severian become
wise as well.

Though Severian's relationships often begin in the
sexist mode—torturer and victim, sex subject and sex object, father-figure and child-figure—they do not remain in
that mode for long.   The torturer becomes his victim, sees
the object as an object for pity rather than for use, is a
comrade to the child.   Why then does Wolfe give us such a
political fright by casting his characters in their original
molds of he-man, moon-goddess, sex-goddess, and child-woman?
First of all, as stereotypes, these characters reflect the
attitudes of the world in which they live.   The world of the
old sun is far from Utopian, and its stereotypes are cruel
and sexist.   People of Severian's society (in contrast to
the Ascians) are by and large pushed into what we now think
of as traditional male/female roles; this is by no means an
unreasonable speculation about the future of an Earth fallen
on hard times.

Second, as archetypes, these characters carry a powerful symbolic and emotional freight from our Greco-Roman and
Judeo-Christian traditions.   Severian, with his sword and
fuligen cape and his profession, begins as the familiar male
figure of cruel death, like those figures of death with his
scythe; when he is transformed into a representation of
Christ, of death with rebirth, the two archetypes of Death
and Messiah evoke in us a strong tradition of emotion and
meaning.   We further remember Diana and Aphrodite and their
avatars when we meet Thecla and Jolenta.   As for Dorcas, her
tradition may have begun with Persephone.

The characters who populate The Book of the New Sun
are meant to be representative figures who direct us to the
tetralogy's meaning.   To reveal that meaning, essentially
Christian, Wolfe uses traditional archetypes of Western
culture; though it is a sexist tradition, it is also an emotionally powerful and aesthetically rich one.   By basing his
characters on the archetypes of this tradition but allowing
them to evolve into more flexible beings, Wolfe takes advantage of the strength of archetypes while avoiding their
potential for rigidity.   The final vision of the tetralogy
is of the New Sun, possible only when humanity has become
humane.   In Severian, who evolves from archetypal male to
representative androgene, the change has occurred.   We see

both the power and the difficulty of that change as it unfolds.

It is clear, then, that The Book quite definitely has substance, not submerged by the tetralogy's baroque style, but incorporated in it. Urth is a representation of our Earth at an undetermined but very distant time in the future. Like any science-fiction speculation, it is not a prediction, but a plausible vision. After "so many centuries of futurity," Earth has been changed by the accretions of time. Her rivers have altered, her sun has dimmed until one can see the stars at midday, and the land itself is so dense with the artifacts of a million years that mining and mountain climbing reveal not geologic but archaeological strata. Our Earth is prehistoric, remembered only in a few hazy myths: of Squanto and a messiah, for instance. The tetralogy concerns only the doings of the Western hemisphere, its action taking place in South America. In this vision, there are vast central governments, the Commonwealth ruling the culturally heterogeneous south and the Ascians controlling seemingly homogeneous North America, the two governments in a state of constant war with one another.

The Commonwealth has a strict caste system, with citizens separated not only by influence and wealth but by physique. The taller and more etiolated the figure, the more aristocratic. The head of the government is the Autarch, or self-ruler; his position is not inherited, and one can proceed from any caste to the autarchy. Most of the government operates independently of the Autarch, whose main functions seem to be to serve as diplomat to extrasolar societies and to search for Urth's salvation in a New Sun to replace the old, dying one.

The Ascians, because they are foreign to Severian, are less completely drawn, but they seem to be ruled by a bureaucracy and are uniformly indoctrinated to group action and group thought; the Ascian ideal is for the individual to be completely submerged into group identity. The story told by the character "Loyal to the Group of Seventeen" shows us that this ideal of a group mind has been only imperfectly realized.

The fauna and flora of Urth are altered from our own through genetic engineering and the introduction of extrasolar species, as well as through the usual processes of extinction and evolution. Technology is an odd mix of the seemingly primitive with the highly advanced. Urth society appears to be labor-intensive, no more technologically sophisticated for the ordinary person in ordinary situations than would have been the case, say, for a person of the fifteenth century. However, the detritus of past technology, such as the rocket ship that houses Severian's guild and the introduced technology of extrasolar societies, such as the weapons which the Commonwealth uses, intrude a level of technical sophistication that might seem magical to many members of the Commonwealth. Thus does Arthur C. Clarke's law, that any technology sufficiently advanced will seem magical, operate.

The speculations that most closely evoke traditional uses of science in science fiction are The Book's military speculations. Wolfe discusses these in his appendix to the fourth volume, "The Aims of the Autarch and the Ships of the Hierodules" and in his chapter, "Cavalry in the Age of the Autarch," from The Castle of the Otter. The appendix notes that Urth technology exists on three levels: the smith level, similar to our historical situation of the fifteenth century, and representative of "the technological ability of the society as a whole"; the Urth level, "the highest technology to be found on the planet, and perhaps in the solar system"; and the stellar level, which represents a level of technology higher than any produced on Urth, and imported by the Hierodules (Appendix, pp. 314-315, CA). The presence of so many levels of technology partly explains the strangeness of the novels' mechanisms of war: everything from swords to lasers and beyond.

Wolfe's other science-fictional explanation for the bizarre differences of The Book's seemingly fantastic battles is the speculation that the "pivotal science of the future will not be . . . mechanical like that of the recent past, nor electronic like that of the present. It will be biological" ("Cavalry in the Age of the Autarch," pp. 52-53, CO). If this is true, then, it becomes scientifically plausible to alter the genetics of animals and even people to form more efficient fighting "machines." And then we understand the presence of destriers, merychips, and arsinoithers; they are not mythical beasts but genetically engineered cavalry animals. Wolfe's use of several levels of technology, and his speculations on a technology not yet very advanced in our time contribute to the tetralogy's aura of fantasy.

Arthur C. Clarke's dictum operates in the realm of military speculation as well. We see the magic in these speculations about greatly advanced technology and categorize the novels as fantasy. In spite of this categorization (volumes from the tetralogy have won two fantasy awards), the novels use the methods of science fiction, employing scientific speculation about the future; however, their use of medieval and Renaissance referents and of themes and archetypes associated with fantasy may suggest the fantastic as well.

What seem more like magic, though they are handled with the science-fictional aim of plausibility, are Wolfe's speculations on time. We have seen similar speculations earlier, especially in "Seven American Nights"; here they are expanded and linked to views of reality and free will, both Platonic and Christian. The tetralogy describes several constructs which alter time in a non-magical way. The Botanical Garden and Father Inere's mirrors, both of which seem to transport people or objects through time, are given a quasi-scientific explanation:

> For a reflected image to exist without an object
> to originate it violates the laws of our
> universe, and therefore an object will be
> brought into existence. (Ch. 20, p. 186, ST)

Though the assumptions behind this explanation have more in common with Borges' story "Tlon, Uqbar, Orbis Tertius" than with modern science, the passage is recognizable as that common science-fictional device, the plausible explanation. The science in science fiction often presents this paradox: it must be offered in a plausible, scientific manner, whether it would hold up to scientific testing and theory or not. This paradoxical view is most noticeable in any science fiction which speculates on time.

The novels discuss time-travel, an accepted motif of science fiction though it has no solid place in the present state of scientific knowledge. The green man from the future and Severian are described as running up and down corridors of time. Master Ash's house is built to exist in several epochs of time, and these strange phenomena of time are given science-fictionally plausible explanations. Time, Master Ash says, is:

> a weaving, a tapestry that extends forever in
> all directions. I follow a thread backward.
> You will trace a color forward, what color I
> cannot know. White may lead you to me, green to
> your green man. (Ch. 17, p. 135, CA)

It has a solidity of existence which makes all eras accessible in some way to all others and so time-travel is possible. Thus the Claw works, as Dorcas explains, by twisting time's fabric:

> when you brought the uhlan back to life it was
> because the Claw twisted time for him to the

89

point at which he still lived. (Ch. 11, pp. 84-
85, SL)

The solidity of time contrasts with the nebulousness of the
world we can see:

> our eyes receive a rain of photons without mass
> or charge from swarming particles like a bil-
> lion, billion suns. . . . From the pattering of
> those photons we believe we see a man. Some-
> times the man we believe we see may be as il-
> lusory as Master Ash or more so. (Ch. 18, p.
> 139, CA)

The insubstantiality of that which can be seen, in contrast
to the solidity of time, that which cannot be seen, has
central thematic importance for The Book. For now, let it
be noted that the presence of an explanation, the use of
words like "photons," puts these speculations on time in the
realm of science fiction.
     Connected with The Book's speculations on time are its
thematic concerns with memory. Because Severian remembers
everything, all the events of his life may be said to
coexist. The alzabo not only captures people but, when it
devours them, it captures their memories, their
personalities—so it captures their existence in time. Both
Severian and the alzabo have power over past time through
memory. Wolfe's earlier views of the power and truth of
memory (in The Fifth Head of Cerberus and Peace, for
example) are confirmed by his view here. Severian forgets
nothing, but that does not mean we can accept his story as
an exact duplication of the reality around him: a perfect
memory does not guarantee a perfectly unprejudiced, totally
conscious, completely sane one. Such filters are part of
the human baggage and therefore inevitably tint Severian's
telling of his story.
     As he recalls his earlier life, the prejudices which
colored his earlier vision return too: the trust in the
rightness of torture, the naive admiration of Vodalus, the
sexist attitude toward women. These are the prejudices of
Severian's culture and upbringing, easy to identify and account for.
     We also know that Severian's total recall applies only
to his conscious life; it extends to his childhood but not
to his origins. In the first volume, he describes his earliest memory, that of a little boy "piling pebbles in the
Old Yard" (Ch. 2, p. 18, ST): later in the tetralogy, he
says he remembers something much earlier:

> I was cold and hungry. I lay upon my back, en-
> circled by brown walls, and heard the sound of
> my own screams. Yes, I must have been an in-
> fant. Not old enough to crawl, I think. (Ch.
> 35, pp. 283-284, CA)

Somehow, the intervening time in his childhood, which would
tell Severian who his parents were, where he came from, has
been forgotten. At various points in Severian's recounting
of his "more than normally turbulent" summer, he loses consciousness and cannot therefore report what has occurred.
Thus we become aware of another imperfection in Severian's
perfect memory.

Both of these causes for unreliability are relatively
easy to gauge. Far more difficult is Severian's knowledge
that his mind may be unbalanced.

> I am in some degree insane. . . . I had lied of-
> ten. . . . Now I could no longer be sure my own
> mind was not lying to me; all my falsehoods were
> recoiling on me, and I who remembered everything
> could not be certain those memories were more
> than my own dreams. (Ch. 3, p. 36, ST)

Nor can we: we must forget any idea of determining what
really happened in some factual sense. With Severian's acknowledgment of his madness, that becomes a futile task; and
even if he were not insane, we could never be certain what
part of his memory was of the waking world, what of his
dreams, any more than we can be sure in ourselves. The difficulty which Wolfe sets up in his tetralogy reminds us that
memory's role is to preserve the past as a story, not as a
document. Memory does not duplicate the past: it gives it
shape, just as fiction shapes a vision and is not meant to
be taken at face value.

Gene Wolfe's fiction is Severian's memoir and both
clarify that the tetralogy is not meant to be taken strictly
at face value. Fiction, like memories, like the world itself, is meant to be delved into for "layers of reality
beneath the reality we see" (Ch. 16, p. 148, ST). Wolfe
and Severian (who compares himself to a wolf in Volume
Three) remind us to interpret their fiction/memoir/world by
telling us several times to do so. The clearest instruction
appears in Chapter 32 of The Shadow of the Torturer, when
Dorcas and Severian discuss the idea that "the universe has
a secret key" (p. 271). In Severian's brown book, which has
a section listing such keys, is one key which claims that:

everything, whatever happens, has three meanings. The first is its practical meaning, what
the book calls 'the thing the plowman sees.'
The second is the reflection of the world about
it. . . . That might be called the soothsayers'
meaning, because it is the one such people use
when they prophesy a fortunate meeting from
tracks of serpents. . . . The third is the transubstantial meaning. Since all objects have
their ultimate origin in the Pancreator, and all
were set in motion by him, so all must express
his will—which is the higher reality. (Ch. 32,
p. 272, ST)

So our world, Severian's memoir, and Wolfe's fiction all
demand such threefold interpretation. It is a notion very
close to the medieval one of quadruplex allegory. There,
each thing, each story had a literal meaning ("what the
plowman sees"), a metaphorical one, an analogical one (these
two are combined in the "soothsayers' meaning"), and an
anagogical one (which corresponds to its "transubstantial
meaning").

Here, in The Book of the New Sun, the practical meaning consists of the story of the young man exiled from his
guild who goes on a quest to return the Claw of the Conciliator. The soothsayers' meaning lies in the tetralogy's
vision of our future. The transubstantial meaning is its
Christian, messianic one. It is to this transubstantial
meaning that so many clues lead us. Many of the repeated
symbols of the tetralogy are associated with Christianity,
the speculations on time harken back to Corinthians, and
Severian is a Christ figure who hopes to save the world from
eternal darkness.

Many of the recurring symbolic images of The Book of
the New Sun are associated directly or indirectly with
Christianity. Holy Katherine, the patronness of the Seekers
for Truth and Penitence, is based on St. Catherine, the
Christian martyr who died on the wheel. She was an educated
aristocrat who was killed by a torturer; she reminds us of
Thecla, and she is mentioned throughout the tetralogy.
Caves and tombs recur throughout as well; Severian enters
them and he escapes them. Among their other associations
(with the female principle, and with ancient mystery
religions, for instance) is their association with the cave
which was Jesus' tomb. The cannibalism of the alzabo
ritual, which results in the gaining of another's memory,
parallels the communion ritual by which the Christian ac-

cepts Jesus into his or her soul through the symbolic par-
taking of Jesus' body and blood. Spring and various other
symbols of rebirth, central to Christianity, among other
religions, occur repeatedly.

These rebirth symbols remind us of the novels' organizing and eponymous symbol, the sun. In The Castle of
the Otter, Wolfe explains the range of this symbol:

> The Book of the New Sun is full of all kinds of
> symbolism. . . . I mentioned the rose symbolism,
> and Roger Stewart just wrote me from Austin,
> Texas mentioning the tree symbolism. But the
> symbol of the sun is central, primary, as the
> titles of both The Book of the New Sun itself
> and The Shadow of the Torturer show.
> (Indirectly, roses and trees are sun symbols
> too. . . .) Urth is dying as the sun gutters;
> its people retain a legend that the Conciliator
> will return and revive the sun, and thus this
> renascent Conciliator is called the New Sun. A
> member of the Seekers for Truth and Penitence
> stands between his victim and the sun . . ., and
> symbolically terminates the life prior to taking
> it. (. . . The Claw of the Conciliator is a
> sun symbol.) ("Sun of Helioscope," pp. 14-15,
> 00)

The sun is figuratively reborn every day; on this future
Urth, people await its literal rebirth. The Conciliator
will be reborn to bring about the miracle and that is why he
is called the New Sun. Like the original Conciliator, the
New Sun must bring moral enlightenment as well as literal.
The Conciliator, the novels make clear, is Christ, the Son.

The Conciliator's power is the power to manipulate
time. That, Dorcas explains, is how the Claw of the Conciliator works, turning back time to the point at which a
victim lives. But, the more we examine such evidence as
Triskele's rescue from the garbage heap well before Severian
found the Claw, the more we realize that the power lies not
in the Claw but in Severian, not in his representation or
symbol but in the Conciliator himself.

Realizing the connection between the Conciliator and
Wolfe's speculations on time, we realize the philosophical
meaning behind the science-fictional one, the transubstantial meaning behind the soothsayers' one. The transubstantial meaning is two-fold. First, it justifies the Christian
and Platonic idea in Corinthians that "the things which are
seen are temporal; but the things which are not seen are

eternal.(4) Second, it allows precognition with free will, another Christian idea, this one associated especially with medieval theology.

To show the applicability of the quotation from Second Corinthians to the tetralogy, let us consider again the notions of time that were discussed earlier. Objects, we are told, can be brought into existence simply to fulfill images in mirrors. The images, then, rather than their objective presence, determine their existence, and thereby their objective existence is relatively unimportant; it is insubstantial. This notion of the insubstantiality of objects is clarified when Severian muses that "from the pattering of those photons we believe we see a man." Objects reflected in mirrors, men we see, are temporary, brought into existence by some outside force, represented only by a pattering of photons, flickering before our sight. "The things which are seen are temporal": temporary, controlled by time. Time itself is solid; compared to a tapestry whose threads can be traced backward and forward, it determines whether objects exist or not, in time, and it determines whether men live or die, in time. Time, which we cannot see, has a substantiality which seen things do not: "the things which are not seen are eternal."

We are meant to extend the list of things that are not seen, of course: it includes Severian's gradual rejection of cruelty and acceptance of compassion and his vision of the holiness of all creation received in "The Sand Garden" (Ch. 31) of The Citadel of the Autarch. These eternal truths, being abstract, are invisible, eternal, and real. Because of their nature, they must be experienced, as the passage of time is experienced, not shown, as objects are. We must live through Severian's experiences, live within his prejudices and experience their alteration, before we can understand what he learns. If it could be seen directly, stated baldly, it would be only temporal. The mazes of elaborate detail in Wolfe's baroque style take on a new necessity: they replicate the way we approach unseeable, eternal ideas.

Time's solidity, its verity, which makes time-travel possible, also explains another Christian belief. How, people have asked, can humanity have free will if God knows all that we will ever do? How can there be precognition with free will? Boethius, a medieval Christian philosopher, answered this question in his Consolation of Philosophy; Gene Wolfe implies the same answer in The Book of the New Sun. Because God sees time all at once, says Boethius, he knows ahead of time how we will choose, and that choice fits his divine plan, but his knowledge doesn't make us choose in a certain way.

The young witch who helps the Cumaean call up the dead in The Claw of the Conciliator offers a similar explanation for the Cumaean's ability to recall the dead and see the future:

> All time exists . . . . If the future did not exist now, how could we journey toward it? If the past does not exist still, how could we leave it behind us? In sleep the mind is encircled by its time, which is why we so often hear the voices of the dead there, and receive intelligence of things to come. Those who have learned to enter the same state while waking live surrounded by their own lives, even as the Abraxas perceives all of time as an eternal instant. (Ch. 31, p. 289, CC)

Because time has permanent, solid existence, then, we choose freely in a world already determined:

> It is in such fashion most sages explain the apparent paradox that though we freely choose to do this or the other, commit some crime or by altruism steal the sacred distinction of the Empyrian, still the Increate commands the entirety and is served equally (that is, totally) by those who would obey and those who would rebel. (Ch. 27, p. 219, SL)

God, having created the world just as he had designed, sees its operation just as he had planned it, though the operators run by their own free will. Severian, not understanding his role in the bringing of the New Sun, nevertheless acts of his own volition, as the Increate planned him to.

These are complex ideas of Christianity, one linked to Platonic notions of the ideal and real versus that which we see, the other coping with the paradox of predeterminism versus free will. They support Wolfe's statement that:

> I am a Catholic, in the real communion-taking sense, which tells you a lot less than you think about my religious beliefs. . . . I believe in God, in the divinity of Christ and in the survival of the person.(5)

95

His notion of a suitable Christ figure, the torturer Severian, also reveals Wolfe's complex and surprising faith. In The Castle of the Otter, Wolfe illuminates his idea of Christ:

> It has been remarked thousands of times that Christ died under torture. Many of us have read so often that he was a "humble carpenter" that we feel a little surge of nausea on seeing the words yet again. But no one ever seems to notice that the instruments of torture were wood, nails, and a hammer; that the man who built the cross was undoubtedly a carpenter too; that the man who hammered in the nails was as much a carpenter as a soldier, as much a carpenter as a torturer. Very few seem even to have noticed that although Christ was a "humble carpenter," the only object we are specifically told he made was not a table or a chair, but a whip.
>
> And if Christ knew not only the pain of torture but the pain of being a torturer (as it seems certain to me that he did) then the dark figure is also capable of being a heroic and even a holy figure, like the black Christs carved in Africa. ("Helioscope," p. 10, CO)

The concept of "taking on the sins of the world" develops more meaning when we imagine Christ suffering not only from the sins of others but from his own sins. Severian, who begins by representing death, becomes a vivimancer, one who brings life. To understand the value of life and to discover eternal ideas of what is good, Severian needs to understand death and evil.

Wolfe makes clear that Severian is a Christ-figure: he raises the dead and is himself raised from the dead in Volume One when struck by the avern, he turns water into wine and is compared to a carpenter or a fisherman, and he suffers spontaneous bleeding as if from a crown of thorns in Volume Two, sees himself as both a child and a man and speculates that he has been given "the attributes of life and light" that will belong to the renewed sun in the fourth volume (Ch.4, p. 277, CA). Because we also understand that Severian will bring the New Sun (though the tetralogy ends before we know for sure), we know that he is the New Sun, the Conciliator reborn. The legends told of the Conciliator make clear that he was Christ, and the Conciliator is repeatedly linked to the New Sun. The circle of associations is complete: Severian, the Conciliator, the New Sun, and Christ.

We know that the millennium which the New Sun will bring includes the material benefits of the physical object, a new sun. And this is of prime importance, as we learn when the image of Master Malrubius asks Severian "which does humanity need more? Justice and peace? Or a New Sun?" Severian replies:

> when a client is driven to the utmost extremity, it is warmth and food and ease from pain he wants. Peace and justice come afterward. (Ch. 31, pp. 246-247, CA)

Severian had earlier expressed his vision of the peace and justice which will follow. Renouncing the torturer's guild for good, as he does when he leaves Thrax in Volume Three, Severian imagines worlds where people

> treated one another as brothers and sisters, worlds where there was no currency but honor, . . . in which the long war between mankind and the beasts was pursued no more. (Ch. 13, pp. 101-102, SL)

This is the Christian peaceable kingdom, ruled by love, compassion, and the connectedness of all creation.

Wolfe's complex, unclichéd, and unsentimental, yet emotionally powerful, Christian vision gives his tetralogy unity and seriousness of purpose. The Book of the New Sun has the literary and theological strength accorded to its predecessors written by those British Christian writers: Tolkien, McDonald, Lewis, and Chesterton.

Three of these four are best known for their fantasies, and such literary genealogy suggests why there has been confusion about whether the tetralogy is fantasy or science fiction. Wolfe himself calls it "science fantasy," which he defines as a story which:

> uses the means of science to achieve the spirit of fantasy. Like fantasy, science fantasy rests upon, and often abounds with, "impossible" creatures and objects. . . . But it uses the methodology of science fiction to show that these things are not only possible but probable.(6)

So Wolfe has butterfly people, giants, and floating islands to make his story seem magical, but he explains how they are probable. Nevertheless, there is more of the "spirit of fantasy" in The Book: its use of a quest story, its archaic terms, the archetypal figures, and finally, the religious theme, which relies on faith rather than proof, on the unseen rather than the seen. Wolfe chose "science fantasy" rather than fantasy for his story, however, to show that such faith is "not only possible but probable."

The Book of the New Sun may be tricky to categorize in a specific way, but it was written by a man who made his reputation as a science-fiction writer and was published as a science-fiction series (through Simon and Schuster's "Timescape" imprint). Whether science fiction, fantasy, or science fantasy, the books come within the provence of the subculture, science fiction. Why is this significant? It has long been a dream of science-fiction writers, readers, and fans that a work of great literature would arise within their subcultural genre. I speculate that The Book of the New Sun is a realization of that dream. It has the depth, richness, and excitement to be The Book of Gold, to be a lasting, luminous, and illuminating work of art. Time will tell.

Is The Book of the New Sun Wolfe's best work? It is certainly his most sustained piece of fine writing. But he is also a master of the short story and the novella, and some of those are, I believe, equally fine--especially "Seven American Nights"--though they do not have, are not meant to have, the scope of a four-volume series of novels. Is the tetralogy the climax to Wolfe's career? Again, time will tell. He has the prospect of many years of writing and growth ahead of him.

NOTES

(1) Colin Greenland, rev. of The Shadow of the Torturer and The Claw of the Conciliator, Foundation, Feb. 1982, pp. 82-85. Elizabeth Hall, rev. of The Book of the New Sun, Extrapolation, 23, No. 3 (1983), pp. 270-274. Algis Budrys, rev. of The Shadow of the Torturer, Magazine of Fantasy and Science Fiction, May 1980, pp. 26-27; rev. of The Claw of the Conciliator, Magazine of Fantasy and Science Fiction, June 1981, pp. 48-51; rev. of The Sword of the Lictor, Magazine of Fantasy and Science Fiction, April 1982, pp. 25-29; and rev. of The Citadel of the Autarch, Magazine of Fantasy and Science Fiction, April 1983, pp. 43-46. John Clute, rev. of The Citadel of the Autarch,

Washington Post Book World, 30 Jan. 1983, 1-2, 11.
Michael Dirda, "Gene Wolfe Talks about 'The Book of the New Sun,'" Washington Post Book World, 30 Jan. 1983, p. 11.

(2) Gerald Jonas, rev. of The Citadel of the Autarch, New York Times Book Review, 22 May 1983, p. 15.

(3) Baird Searles, rev. of The Citadel of the Autarch, Isaac Asimov's Science Fiction Magazine, May 1983, p. 167.

(4) The Bible, Second Corinthians, Ch. 4, v. 18.

(5) Joan Gordon, "An Interview with Gene Wolfe, Science Fiction Review, Summer 1981, p. 18.

(6) Gene Wolfe, "What Do They Mean, SF?," The Writer, Aug. 1980, p. 13.

IX

COMPLETE ANNOTATED BIBLIOGRAPHY OF FICTION
CITED BY FIRST EDITIONS
THROUGH 1983

"The Adopted Father." Isaac Asimov's Science Fiction
Magazine, Dec. 1980, pp. 117-125. The isolated child
meets an isolated father.
"Against the Lafayette Escadrille." In Again Dangerous Vi-
sions. Ed. Harlan Ellison. Garden City, NY:
Doubleday, 1972, pp. 129-131. Second of three stories
published as "Mathoms from the Time Closet" (with
"Robot's Story" and "Loco Parentis"): duplicating the
past brings it back.
"Alien Stones." In Orbit 11. Ed. Damon Knight. New York:
Putnam, 1972, pp. 7-43. Alien linguistics and in-
verted science-fiction conventions.
"An Article About Hunting." In Saving Worlds. Ed. Roger
Elwood and Virginia Kidd. Garden City, NY:
Doubleday, 1973, pp. 93-103. An ecology story from
the point of view of a bureaucrat.
"Beautyland." In Saving Worlds. Ed. Roger Elwood and Vir-
ginia Kidd. Garden City, NY: Doubleday, 1973, pp.
183-188. Another ecology story, from the point of
view of a destroyer.
"Beech Hill." In Infinity Three. Ed. Robert Hoskins. New
York: Lancer, 1972, pp. 84-91. A man escapes his
shabby life for a vacation in which fantasies are
lived out.
"The Blue Mouse." In Many Worlds of SF. Ed. Ben Bova. New
York: Dutton, 1971, pp. 6-22. A future war story
with uncharacteristic emphasis on technology.
"Car Sinister." The Magazine of Fantasy and Science Fiction, Jan. 1970, pp. 57-63. A punning entertainment.
"The Changeling." In Orbit 3. Ed. Damon Knight. New York:
Berkley, 1968, pp. 109-123. The isolated child in a
story which presages the novel Peace.
"Cherry Jubilee." Isaac Asimov's Science Fiction Magazine,
19 Jan. 1982, pp. 108-135. A science-fiction mystery
with twins.
The Citadel of the Autarch. New York: Simon and Schuster,
1982. Fourth volume of the tetralogy, The Book of the
New Sun.
"Civis Laputus Sum." In Dystopian Visions. Ed. Roger Elwood. Englewood Cliffs, NJ: Prentice Hall, 1975, pp.
46-54. Moby Dick on a floating island after the books
have been burned.

The Claw of the Conciliator. New York: Simon and Schuster,
    1981. Second volume of the tetralogy, *The Book of the
    New Sun*.
"Continuing Westward." In *Orbit 12*. Ed. Damon Knight. New
    York: Putnam, 1973, pp. 204-209. A time paradox
    story set in North Africa.
"A Criminal Proceeding." In *Interfaces*. Ed. Ursula K.
    LeGuin and Virginia Kidd. New York: Ace, 1980, pp.
    107-214. Takes the televising of courtroom proceed-
    ings to a bizarre extreme.
"Cues." In *The Far Side of Time*. Ed. Roger Elwood. New
    York: Dodd Mead, 1973, pp. 145-150. An entertainment
    about comedians and aliens.
"The Dark of the June." In *Continuum 1*. Ed. Roger Elwood.
    New York: Putnam, 1974, pp. 158-165. First of four
    connected *Continuum* stories (with "The Death of Hyle,"
    "From the Notebook of Dr. Stein," and "Thag"), this is
    about a runaway girl.
"The Dead Man." *Sir*, Oct. 1965, pp. 13, 61-62. Wolfe's
    first published story, a ghost story about India.
"The Death of Doctor Island." In *Universe 3*. Ed. Terry
    Carr. New York: Random House, 1973, pp. 3-69.
    Second of the "Island of Doctor Death" trilogy (with
    "The Island of Doctor Death and Other Stories" and
    "The Doctor of Death Island"), a Nebula Award winner
    with an adolescent isolato.
"The Death of Hyle." In *Continuum 2*. Ed. Roger Elwood.
    New York: Putnam, 19174, pp. 181-188. Second in the
    Continuum series (with "The Dark of the June," "From
    the Notebook of Dr. Stein," and "Thag"): the father
    seeks his daughter.
"The Detective of Dreams." In *Dark Forces*. Ed. Kirby
    McCauley. New York: Viking, 1980, pp. 196-213. A
    Dickensian tale with a Christian theme.
The Devil in a Forest. Chicago: Follett, 1976. An adoles-
    cent historical novel with a religious theme.
"The Doctor of Death Island." In *Immortal: Short Novels of
    the Transhuman Future*." Ed. Jack Dann. New York:
    Harper and Row, 1978, pp. 57-110. Third in the
    "Island of Doctor Death" series (with "The Island of
    Doctor Death and Other Stories" and "The Death of Doc-
    tor Island"), with an adult isolato.
"Eyebem." In *Orbit 7*. Ed. Damon Knight. New York: Put-
    nam, 1970, pp. 67-78. Examining the nature of
    humanity through robots.
"The Eyeflash Miracles." In *Future Power*. Ed. Gardner
    Dozois and Jack Dann. New York: Random House, 1976,
    pp. 175-250. A novella with a transcendent isolato.

"Feather Tigers." In Edge (New Zealand Quarterly), Fall-Winter 1973, pp. 52-56. Adorable yet sinister alien invaders and the effect of the mind on the world around it.

"The Fifth Head of Cerberus." In Orbit 10. Ed. Damon Knight. New York: Putnam, 1972, pp. 9-79. A coming-of-age story that begins The Fifth Head of Cerberus novella cycle.

The Fifth Head of Cerberus. New York: Scribners, 1972. Contains "The Fifth Head of Cerberus," "'A Story,' by John V. Marsch," and "V.R.T," a novella cycle which made a strong contribution to Wolfe's reputation as a craftsman.

"Folia's Story: The Armiger's Daughter." Amazing, Nov. 1982, pp. 48-54. One of the embedded stories of Citadel of the Autarch (her real name is Foila).

"Forlesen." In Orbit 14. Ed. Damon Knight. New York: Harper and Row, 1974, pp. 160-200. Kafka-esque bureaucrat in a surreal work-day.

"Four Wolves." Amazing, May 1983, pp. 79-84. A story that may be about the writing of The Book of the New Sun.

"From the Desk of Gilmer C. Merton." The Magazine of Fantasy and Science Fiction, June 1983, pp. 117-121. An epistilary werewolf entertainment.

"From the Notebook of Dr. Stein." In Continuum 3. Ed. Roger Elwood. New York: Putnam, 19174, pp. 137-144. Third in the Continuum series (with "The Dark of the June," "The Death of Hyle," and "Thag"), this with a disturbed and possessed girl.

Gene Wolfe's Book of Days. Garden City, NY: Doubleday, 1981. Collection of short fiction which contains: "How the Whip Came Back," "Of Relays and Roses," "Paul's Treehouse," "St. Brandon," "Beautyland," "Car Sinister," "The Blue Mouse," "How I Lost the Second World War and Turned Back the German Invasion," "The Adopted Father," "Forlesen," "An Article about Hunting," "The Changeling," "Many Mansions," "Against the Lafayette Escadrille," "Three Million Square Miles," "The War Beneath the Tree," "La Befana," and "Melting."

"The God and His Man." Isaac Asimov's Science Fiction Magazine, Feb. 1980, pp. 20-25. Written in a Biblical style, this story might be an allegory of the Urth of The Book of the New Sun.

"Going to the Beach." In Showcase. Ed. Roger Elwood. New York: Harper and Row, 1973, pp. 165-172. The nature of humanity examined in relationships between human and android.

"The Green Wall Said." <u>New Worlds</u>, Aug. 1967, pp. 26-27.
   Crossed communications and the value of humanity.
"The Headless Man." In <u>Universe 2</u>. Ed. Terry Carr. New
   York: Ace, 1972, pp. 211-218. A grotesque man finds
   company.
"The Hero as Werwolf." <u>New Improved Sun</u>. Ed. Thomas Disch.
   New York: Harper and Row, 1975, pp. 182-200. Twisted
   science-fiction conventions to examine the nature of
   humanity.
"The HORARS of War." In <u>Nova 1</u>. Ed. Harry Harrison. New
   York: Delacorte, 1970, pp. 82-101. A war story ex-
   amining the nature of humanity through the use of
   androids.
"Hour of Trust." In <u>Bad Moon Rising</u>. Ed. Thomas Disch.
   New York: Harper and Row, 1973, pp. 167-202. War be-
   tween corporations and radicals.
"House of Ancestors." <u>IF</u>, June 1968, pp. 101-120. An early
   handling of the architecture of memory.
"How I Lost the Second World War and Helped Turn Back the
   German Invasion." <u>Analog</u>, May 1973, pp. 83-95. An
   alternate world entertainment.
"How the Whip Came Back." In <u>Orbit 6</u>. Ed. Damon Knight.
   New York: Putnam, 1970, pp. 55-74. The effect on
   humanity and humaneness of the master/slave relation-
   ship.
"In Looking-Glass Castle." <u>Triquarterly 49</u>. Fall 1980, pp.
   117-129. The war between men and women taken
   literally.
"The Island of Doctor Death and Other Stories." In <u>Orbit 7</u>.
   Ed. Damon Knight. New York: Putnam, 1970, pp. 199-
   217. First in the "Island of Doctor Death" novella
   series (with "The Death of Doctor Island" and "The
   Doctor of Death Island"): the isolato is a child.
<u>The Island of Doctor Death and Other Stories and Other
   Stories</u>. New York: Pocket, 1980. Short fiction collection containing: "The Island of Doctor Death and
   Other Stories," "Alien Stones," "La Befana," "The Hero
   as Werwolf," "Three Fingers," "The Death of Doctor Is-
   land," "Feather Tigers," "Hour of Trust," "Tracking
   Song," "The Toy Theater," "The Doctor of Death Is-
   land," "Cues," "The Eyeflash Miracles," and "Seven
   American Nights."
"It's Very Clean." In <u>Generation</u>. Ed. David Gerrold. New
   York: Delacorte, 1972, pp. 73-78. Who is real and
   who is not, in the sexual arena.
"Kevin Malone." In <u>New Terrors</u>. Ed. Ian Campbell. London:
   Pan, 1980, pp. 173-184. An isolato's search for home
   requires unwitting actors.

"King Under the Mountain." IF, Nov./Dec. 1970, pp. 86-90.
   A personal relationship between a man and a computer.
"La Befana." Galaxy, Jan. 1973, pp. 72-76. An Italian
   Christmas legend travels to the future on another
   planet.
"Last Day." In Speculations. Ed. Issac Asimov and Alice
   Laurance. Boston: Houghton Mifflin, 1982, pp. 135-
   139. The relationship between humans and machines.
"The Last Thrilling Wonder Story." Isaac Asimov's Science
   Fiction Magazine, June 1982, pp. 144-169. A metafic-
   tional conversation between author and square-jawed
   hero.
"Loco Parentis." In Again, Dangerous Visions. Ed. Harlan
   Ellison. Garden City, NY: Doubleday, 1972, pp. 132-
   133. Third of three stories published as "Mathoms
   from the Time Closet" (with "Robot's Story" and
   "Against the Lafayette Escadrille"): are parents
   machines for nurturing?
"Many Mansions." In Orbit 19. Ed. Damon Knight. New York:
   Harper and Row, 1977, pp. 355-44. The architecture of
   memory and the strength of nostalgia.
"The Marvelous Brass Chessplaying Automaton." In Universe
   7. Ed. Terry Carr. Garden City NY: Doubleday, 1977,
   pp. 113-133. Humanity versus machines.
"Melting." In Orbit 15. Ed. Damon Knight. New York: Harper and Row, 1974, pp. 93-98. An evaporating time-
   travel cocktail party.
"A Method Bit in 'B.'" In Orbit 8. Ed. Damon Knight. New
   York: Putnam, 1970, pp. 179-183. A method actor in a
   'b' movie for whom the movie is reality.
"Morning Glory." In Alchemy and Academe. Ed. Anne McCaf-
   frey. Garden City, NY: Doubleday, 1970, pp. 170-177.
   Intelligence and therapy in people and plants.
"Mountains Like Mice." IF, May 1966, pp. 81-96. Wolfe's
   first published science-fiction story, this is an in-
   itiation story showing his characteristic interest in
   myth.
"Of Relays and Roses." IF, Sept./Oct. 1970, pp. 161-170,
   and 182. Computer matchmaking versus corporate ef-
   ficiency.
Operation ARES. New York: Berkley, 1970. Wolfe's first
   published novel, political science-fiction preaching
   rugged individualism.
"Our Neighbor, by David Copperfield." In Rooms of Paradise.
   Ed. Lee Harding. Melbourne: Quartet, 1978, pp. 71-
   83. A Dickensian tale about mesmerism.
"The Packerhaus Method." In Infinity I. Ed. Robert Hoskins. New York: Lancer, 1970, pp. 111-117. a

104

futuristic twist on "Arsenic and Old Lace."

"Paul's Treehouse." In Orbit 5. Ed. Damon Knight. New York: Putnam, 1969, pp. 129-137. Parents and children during the coming revolution.

Peace. New York: Harper and Row, 1975. Wolfe's mainstream novel in the form of a memoir with embedded stories.

"Peritonitis." In Tomorrow's Alternatives. Ed. Roger Elwood. New York: Macmillan, 1973, pp. 65-71. From the viewpoint of the germs.

"The Recording." The Magazine of Fantasy and Science Fiction, April 19712, pp. 97-100. An old man remembers his childhood selfishness without gaining self-knowledge.

"Remembrance to Come." In Orbit 6. Ed. Damon Knight. New York: Putnam, 1970, pp. 40-53. A professor in a Proustian future.

"Robot's Story." In Again, Dangerous Visions. Ed. Harlan Ellison. Garden City, NY: Doubleday, 19172, pp. 126-134. First of three stories published as "Mathoms from the Time Closet" (with "Against the Lafayette Escadrille" and "Loco Parentis"): a boy who thinks he's a robot tells a story about a man treated like one.

"The Rubber Bend." In Universe 5. Ed. Terry Carr. New York: Random House, 1974, pp. 139-163. Humans and robots in a Sherlock Holmes mystery: a sequel to "Slaves of Silver."

"St. Brandon." In Gene Wolfe's Book of Days. Garden City, NY: Doubleday, 1981, pp. 35-42. An Irish tale excerpted from Peace.

"Screen Test." Mike Shane's Mystery Magazine, July 1967, pp. 141-144. A non-science-fiction mystery story based on false assumptions.

"Seven American Nights." In Orbit 20. Ed. Damon Knight. New York: Harper and Row, 1978, pp. 175-233. A complex novella about time, humanity, and empathy.

The Shadow of the Torturer. New York: Simon and Schuster, 1980. The first volume of the acclaimed tetralogy, The Book of the New Sun.

"Silhouette." In New Atlantis. Ed. Robert Silverberg. New York: Hawthorn, 1975, pp. 1-56. An isolato grapples with the meaning of reality and humanity.

"Slaves of Silver." IF, March/April 1971, pp. 68-83. First of two Sherlock Holmesian mysteries featuring a robot Dr. Watson (see also "The Rubber Bend").

"A Solar Labyrinth." The Magazine of Fantasy and Science Fiction, April 1983, pp. 50-52. A Borgesian maze.

"Sonya, Crane Wessleman, and Kittee." In Orbit 8. Ed.

Damon Knight. New York: Putnam, 1970, pp. 86-91. A light treatment of the nature of humanity.

"Straw." Galaxy, Jan. 1975, pp. 117-128. A young mercenary in an alternate medieval Europe.

"Suzanne Delage." In Edges. Ed. Ursula L. Le Guin and Virginia Kidd. New York: Pocket, 1980, pp. 93-98. An isolated man's search for the extraordinary.

"Sweet Forest Maid." The Magazine of Fantasy and Science Fiction, July 1971, pp. 60-64. An isolated woman searches for the Abominable Snowwoman and the question of the natu e of humanity is raised.

The Sword of the Lictor. New York: Simon and Schuster, 1981. The third volume of The Book of the New Sun.

"The Tale of the Student and His Son." The Magazine of Fantasy and Science Fiction, Oct. 1981, pp. 117-128. An embedded story from The Citadel of the Autarch.

"Tarzan of the Grapes," The Magazine of Fantasy and Science Fiction, June 1972, pp. 123-129. Newsmen invent a hippie myth that comes true.

"Thag." In Continuum 4. Ed. Roger Elwood. New York: Putnam, 1975. Fourth in the Continuum series and the most fantastic (see also "The Dark of the June," "The Death of Hyle," and "From the Notebook of Dr. Stein").

"Thou Spark of Blood." IF, April 1970, pp. 105-109, and 157. A spaceship murder with allusions to Macbeth.

"Three Fingers." In New Constellations. Ed. Thomas Disch and Charles Naylor. New York: Harper and Row, 1976, pp. 5-12. A sinister view of Walt Disney's creatures.

"Three Million Square Miles." In Ruins of Earth. Ed. Thomas Disch. New York: Putnam, 1971, pp. 39-44. An ecological story: looking for America's wilderness.

"To the Dark Tower Came." In Orbit 19. Ed. Damon Knight. New York: Harper and Row, 1977, pp. 120-125. An ambiguous story packed with allusions to everyone from King Lear to "Jack and the Beanstalk."

"The Toy Theater." In Orbit 9. Ed. Damon Knight. New York: Putnam, 1971, pp. 43-50. Examines the nature of humanity and the value of reality, with puppets.

"Tracking Song." In In the Wake of Man. Ed. Roger Elwood. New York: Bobbs Merrill, 1975, pp. 87-176. Examines the nature of humanity.

"Trip Trap." In Orbit 2. Ed. Damon Knight. New York: Berkley, 1967, pp. 110-144. Early exploration of nature of humanity using myths and a human archaeologist.

"Volksweapon." Mike Shane's Mystery Magazine, Sept. 1967, pp. 53-59. A straight mystery story.

"The War Beneath the Tree." Omni, Dec. 1979, pp. 822-284,

130. A lonely boy and his rejected toys at Christmas.
"Westwind." IF, July/Aug. 1973, pp. 110-117. The best
leader for lonely people makes it a personal relation-
ship.
"When I Was Ming the Merciless." In Ides of Tomorrow. Ed.
Terry Carr. Boston: Little Brown, 1976, pp. 127-136.
Confused identities in a student exercise/rebellion.
The Wolfe Archipelago. Willimantic, Conn: Ziesing
Brothers, 1983. Collects the "Island of Dr. Death"
trilogy with, in its Foreword, a companion, "Death of
the Island Doctor."
"The Woman the Unicorn Loved." Isaac Asimov's Science Fic-
tion Magazine, June 1980, pp. 70-87. Mythology and
genetic engineering: a sequel to "The Woman Who Loved
the Centaur Pholus" (see below).
"The Woman Who Loved the Centaur Pholus." Isaac Asimov's
Science Fiction Magazine, Dec. 1979, pp. 108-118.
Mythology and genetic engineering (see also "The Woman
the Unicorn Loved," above).

X

A SELECTED AND ANNOTATED BIBLIOGRAPHY
OF NON-FICTION WRITING

"The Bellman's Wonder Ring." In Clarion SF. Ed. Kate Wilhelm. New York: Berkley, 1977, pp. 43-47. Wolfe ponders the difficulty of teaching professionalism in writing.

Castle of the Otter: A Book About the Book of the New Sun. Willimantic, Conn: Ziesing Brothers, 1982. Eleven chapters on the making of Wolfe's trilogy, ranging in subjects from vocabulary through symbols to reviews; includes a "bio-bibliography" by Gordon Benson, Jr.

"More Translations from the Editorial." The Alien Critic, No. 9 (May 1974), pp. 32-33. Wolfe speaks in his role as an editor of Plant Engineering.

"Organizing a Life to Write." Empire SF, 4, No. 2 (Feb. 1979), 25-26; rpt. Empire, No. 9 (1977). The nature and sacrifices of the serious writer.

"The Tolkien toll-free fifties freeway to Mordor and points beyond hurray!" Vector, 67/8. pp. 7-11. An interpretation of The Lord of the Rings.

"What Do They Mean, SF?" The Writer, August 1980, pp. 11-13, and 45. Wolfe defines science fiction, speculative fiction, and science fantasy.

"Writers' Conferences" (with George R.R. Martin). Empire SF, No. 14 (July 1978), pp. 11-14. A conversation recorded at B'Hamacon in Birmingham, Alabama, in August, 1977, discussing the merits of writers' conferences.

XI

A SELECTED AND ANNOTATED SECONDARY BIBLIOGRAPHY

Bishop, Michael. "Gene Wolfe as Hero." Thrust, N. 16 (Fall 1980), pp. 10-13. Claiming Wolfe as a hero who would "never publish a bad book," Bishop lauds The Shadow of the Torturer, discusses Wolfe's characteristic style, and asks Wolfe some questions about The Book of the New Sun.

Budrys, Algis. Rev. of The Shadow of the Torturer. The Magazine of Fantasy and Science Fiction, May 1980, pp. 26-27. Sees The Book of the New Sun not as a series of books but as "one book with four aspects."

_____. Rev. of The Claw of the Conciliator. The Magazine of Fantasy and Science Fiction, June 1981, pp. 48-51. Discusses The Book's fine craftsmanship.

_____. Rev. of The Sword of the Lictor. The Magazine of Fantasy and Science Fiction, April 1982, pp. 25-29. Discusses The Book's categorization as science fiction and The Sword of the Lictor as a transitional volume.

_____. Rev. of The Citadel of the Autarch. The Magazine of Fantasy and Science Fiction, April 1983, pp. 43-46. Calling the completion of the tetralogy "a major event in this field," Budrys speculates upon whether The Book is "a true masterwork, or . . . a work that gives the impression of being a masterwork."

Clute, John. Rev. of The Citadel of the Autarch. Washington Post Book World, 30 Jan. 1983, pp. 1-2, and 11. This highly favorable review touches upon The Book's religious themes.

Dirda, Michael. "Gene Wolfe Talks About 'The Book of the New Sun.'" Washington Post Book World, 30 Jan. 1983, p. 11. A general interview with some interesting discussion of influences.

Dozois, Gardner. "An Interview of Gene Wolfe." Xenolith One, pp. 26-34. A discussion of Wolfe's goals as a writer.

Edwards, Malcolm. "Gene Wolfe: an Interview." Vector, No. 6, (May-June 1973), pp. 7-15. Some autobiographical information, along with discussions of Mervyn Peake and of Wolfe's writing schedule.

_____. "Wolfe, Gene." The Science Fiction Encyclopedia. Ed. Peter Nicholls. Garden City, NY: Doubleday, 1979, pp. 659-660. Good summary of Wolfe's career and characteristics.

Gordon, Joan. "An Interview with Gene Wolfe." Science Fiction Review, Summer 1981, pp. 18-22. Wolfe discusses his life, his writing, writing in general, and life in general.

Greenland, Colin. Rev. of The Shadow of the Torturer and The Claw of the Conciliator. Foundation, Feb. 1982, pp. 82-85. Intelligent discussion of Wolfe's use of science fiction and fantasy, and of the layers of his prose.

Hull, Elizabeth. Rev. of The Book of the New Sun. Extrapolation, 23, No. 3 (1983), 270-274. Stresses the importance of The Book of the New Sun in science fiction and discusses the functions of the four volumes.

Jonas, Gerald. Rev. of The Citadel of the Autarch. New York Times Book Review, 22 May 1983, p. 15. Significant because the highly favorable review represents the New York Times's prestigious acknowledgment of Wolfe's standing in science fiction.

Kaveney, Roz. Rev. of The Island of Doctor Death and Other Stories. Foundation, 21 (Feb. 1981), pp. 79-83. Kaveney offers interpretations of several short stories and discusses several recurring patterns.

Sargent, Pamela. Afterword to The Fifth Head of Cerberus. New York: Ace, 1976, pp. 271-277. Discussion of the novella cycle's unity.

_____. "Wolfe, Gene (Rodman)." Twentieth Century Science Fiction Writers. Ed. Curtis C. Smith. NY: St. Martins, 1981, pp. 595-596. Includes an interesting quote from Wolfe about his writing; Sargent summarizes his major work through The Fifth Head of Cerberus.

INDEX

Greene, Graham: 19
Greenland, Colin: 73, 110
"Hallvard's Story--The Two Sealers": 80
"Headless Man, The": 103
Heinlein, Robert: 8, 11
"Hero as Werwolf, The": 51, 57, 58, 103
historical novel: 46-48, 101
"HORARS of War, The": 54, 103
"Hour of Trust": 103
"House of Ancestors": 29, 54, 103
"How I Lost the Second World War and Turned Back the German
    Invasion": 5, 52-53, 102, 103
"How the Whip Came Back": 102, 103
Hugo Award: 9, 51, 73
Hull, Elizabeth: 73, 110
humanity, nature of: 19, 20, 22-23, 24, 29, 64-67, 101,
    102, 103, 105, 106
identity: 7, 19, 20, 24, 27, 29, 107
"In Looking-Glass Castle": 103
"Island of Doctor Death and Other Stories, The": 7, 29, 30,
    51, 58, 59, 60-62, 101, 103
Island of Doctor Death and Other Stories and Other Stories,
    The: 6, 51, 103, 110
"Island of Doctor Death, The" trilogy: 20, 51, 54, 59, 60-
    63, 101, 103
isolation: 7, 29, 32, 35-36, 39, 44, 49, 58-64, 100, 101,
    102, 103, 105, 106, 107
"It's Very Clean": 103
Jonas, Gerald: 74, 110
Kafka, Franz: 6, 102
Kaveney, Roz: 110
"Kevin Malone": 103
"King Under the Mountain": 103
Knight, Damon: 6, 9, 17, 19
Korean War: 4, 59-60
"La Befana": 6, 102, 103, 104
"Last Day": 104
"Last Thrilling Wonder Story, The": 51, 72, 104
Lewis, C. S.: 61, 97
"Loco Parentis": 100, 104, 105
Locus: 9, 73
"Loyal to the Group of Seventeen's Story--the Just Man":
    80, 81, 87
McDonald, George: 97
mainstream fiction: 30-31
"Many Mansions": 23, 51, 53, 102, 104
"The Marvelous Brass Chessplaying Automaton": 104
"Mathoms from the Time Closet": 100, 104, 105

114

"Rubber Bend, The": 105
"St. Brandon": 102, 105
Sargent, Pamela: 19, 110
science fantasy: 97-98, 108
science fiction: 3, 8, 13, 20, 30-31, 41, 46-47, 58, 69-70,
     75, 87, 88-90, 98, 108, 109, 110
"Screen Test": 105
Searles, Baird: 74
sentence structure: 7, 45-46, 76-77
setting: 19, 23, 44, 80-81
"Seven American Nights": 7, 8, 20, 41, 51, 67-72, 89, 98,
     103, 105
Severian: 8, 49-50, 82-86, 90-92
Shadow of the Torturer, The: 8, 9, 58, 73-98, 105, 109, 110
"Silhouette": 105
"Slaves of Silver": 105
Slepyan, Norbert: 19
sociological stories: 6, 15, 53-54
"A Solar Labyrinth": 105
"Sonya, Crane Wessleman, and Kittee": 106
speculative fiction: 3, 8, 31, 59, 108
story cycle: 20, 28, 60
storytelling: 27-28, 38-39, 80
"Straw": 58, 106
style: 6, 7, 12, 13, 28, 37, 44-46, 75-81, 109
sun: 93
"Suzanne Delage": 106
"Sweet Forest Maid": 106
Sword of the Lictor, The: 73-98, 106, 109
"Tale of the Boy Called Frog, The": 79
"Tale of the Student and His Son, The": 79, 106
"Tarzan of the Grapes": 106
"Thag": 51, 101, 102, 106
"Thag" series: 20, 51, 72, 101, 102, 106
"Thou Spark of Blood": 106
"Three Fingers": 57, 58, 103, 106
"Three Million Square Miles": 30, 53, 102, 106
time: 41-42, 69-70, 76, 89-90, 93-95, 100, 101, 104, 105
"To the Dark Tower Come": 72, 106
Tolkien, J.R.R.: 97, 108
"The Tolkien toll-free fifties freeway to Mordor and points
     beyond hurray!": 108
totems: 64-65
"Toy Theater": 29, 51, 64, 103, 106
"Tracking Song": 7, 20, 51, 64-66, 103, 106
"Trip Trap": 64, 106
Urth of the New Sun, The: 73
"Volksweapon": 106